JULIUS CAESAR

HARCOURT SHAKESPEARE

JULIUS CAESAR
SECOND EDITION

Series Editor: Ken Roy

edited by
Ken Roy and Allan Patenaude

THOMSON

NELSON

Canadian Cataloguing in Publication Data

Shakespeare, William, 1564–1616
    Julius Caesar

(Harcourt Shakespeare)
2nd ed.
ISBN 0-7747-0577-9

1. Caesar, Julius—Drama. I. Patenaude, Allan. II. Title. III. Series.

PR2808.A2P37 1999   822.3'3   C99-930656-1

Harcourt Shakespeare Series Editor: Ken Roy

Project Manager: Gaynor Fitzpatrick
Developmental Editor: Jane Clark
Editorial Assistant: Ian Nussbaum
Production Editor: Jinnean Barnard
Production Coordinator: Tanya Mossa
Copy Editor: Maraya Raduha
Cover and Interior Design: Michael van Elsen Design Inc.
Page Composition: Carolyn Hutchings
Cover and Text Illustration: Laszlo and Marika Gal
Title Logotype: Sonya V. Thursby/Opus House
Printing and Binding: Kromar Printing Ltd.

Nelson
1120 Birchmount Road
Toronto, Ontario M1K 5G4
1-800-668-0671
www.nelson.com

Printed in Canada
2 3 4 5   08 07 06 05

To the Reader

You may already know something about the play *Julius Caesar*—it is referred to often in newscasts in the context of current politics, and lines from it are frequently quoted.

This play can teach us a great deal about ourselves: it is filled with omens, portents, and dreams that seem to shape the reactions and futures of its major participants. While some people believe that *Julius Caesar* is a play about power, others believe it is a play about love: love of country, love of self, love of ideals; some believe it is about freedom, while others believe it is about anarchy; still others believe it is a play about human ego gone mad. As you experience the play, you will be prompted to examine where *you* stand on these issues.

However, *Julius Caesar* is not just a political play; it is about character, and Brutus is its focus. It is a complex and ambiguous play that goes well beyond politics and into the realm of human behaviour and motivation.

The text of a play provides the material for creating drama on stage. The language of the text inspires directors, actors, designers, technicians, and audiences to create together their sense of the play. Through activities provided in this edition of *Julius Caesar*, you have many opportunities to participate in the process of creating your own sense of the play.

Before reading the scenes, you will be invited to discuss thoughts and experiences similar to ones the characters will encounter. Following scenes and acts, you will have the opportunity to explore some of the ideas, themes, and feelings you experienced while reading the text, as you complete selected activities. Your personal responses and reactions to the scenes and acts will provide the starting points for working through the activities. Your first impressions are always important.

Some of the activities ask you to consider the text through the eyes of a director. Others invite you to see the play through an actor's or designer's eyes. Many encourage you to bring your own experiences to events and circumstances that, although they happened many centuries ago, have significance for today's audiences.

At times you may choose to work alone as you complete chosen activities and at other times with one or several partners. Frequently, you will need to return to the text as you develop and/or confirm initial responses to the scenes in which you are participating. In doing so, you will be using this edition of *Julius Caesar* in the way for which it is intended—as a springboard for creative involvement.

Getting Started

We live in a country where we enjoy the benefits of a political system that is democratic—government by the people for the people. Of course, this form of government is not found in every country in the world today, nor has it always been the system of rule throughout history. One focus of *Julius Caesar* is that of government and its leadership. Some of the questions that arise in the development of this play are the following:

- What constitutes leadership?
- What qualifies a person to seek or assume leadership?
- How should leadership be attained and maintained?
- What should be the relationship between the leadership of a government and the people it governs?

The play has other main ideas such as friendship, partnership, superstition, jealousy, fear, ambition, social order and revolution, power, and citizenship—ideas familiar to us because we too are a part of the same humanity that William Shakespeare wrote about in his plays.

Before you explore the drama of *Julius Caesar*, you may wish to discuss some of the questions and themes presented in this play. This will give you a good opportunity to begin writing in your journal. Record what you think are some of the important and interesting points that were made in your discussions. These thoughts and opinions will become reference points for you as you select activities to complete following the various scenes and acts in this play. You might consider the following questions for discussion and for journal writing responses as well.

1. What are the five most important qualities a political leader of a country needs? Why is it necessary for him or her to possess each of these?

2. In Canada, what provisions exist for the political opponents of the party in power to express themselves?

3. Many countries in the world are suffering or have suffered from social and political unrest. Choose one of these countries and situations to discuss. Explain the causes and events of the political unrest to your group. If you were the country's political leader, what might you do to quell the unrest?

4. Think of a contemporary or historical person who has dedicated his or her life to a cause.

   • What difficulties did he or she encounter while promoting the cause?
   • What were the results of his or her efforts?
   • Did the person experience any failures in representing the cause? If so, how did he or she handle them?
   • What successes did the person achieve?

   Talk about your ideas. If necessary, do some research to support your information.

5. *Julius Caesar* is set in early Roman times. The society of that time was in many ways an advanced one. With the assistance of your teacher and/or librarian, research some of the influences that Roman society has had on our modern world. Share your findings with other members of your group.

6. What characteristics do you associate with "ambitious" people? Describe the qualities that an ambitious person you know possesses. Are you attracted to the person? Why or why not?

7. How do you think modern political leaders in Canada make their government-related decisions? Who are some of the people they might consult? If you were leader of a Canadian political party, whose counsel would you seek before making a decision that might affect the social and economic welfare of the people?

Dramatis Personae
(Characters in the Play)

Julius Cæsar, a conquering Roman general

His followers:
Calpurnia, Julius Cæsar's wife
Marcus Antonius (Mark Antony), a Roman general loyal
  to Cæsar (also related to him)
Octavius Cæsar, a military leader and Cæsar's grand-
  nephew, whom Cæsar named as his successor

Marcus Brutus, a general and Roman of stature; formerly a
  supporter of Pompey, Rome's previous ruler, Brutus
  was later pardoned and befriended by Cæsar.
Cassius, a noble Roman and the driving force behind the
  conspirators

Their followers:
Portia, Brutus's wife
Casca
Trebonius
Ligarius   conspirators
Decius Brutus
Metellus Cimber
Cinna
Titinius   noted generals and friends
Messala   of Brutus and Cassius
Lucilius
Young Cato   friends of Brutus
Volumnius   and Cassius
Pindarus, servant to Cassius
Varro
Clitus
Claudius   soldiers or servants
Strato   of Brutus
Lucius
Dardanius

(continued)

Dramatis Personae *(continued)*
(Characters in the Play)

Other Romans:

Lepidus (Marcus Æmilius), supported Mark Antony after Cæsar's murder; later a part of the ruling Second Triumvirate

Cicero
Publius } senators
Popilius Lena

Artemidorus, a rhetorician (a skilled speaker)

Flavius and **Marullus,** tribunes elected to protect the rights of the common people

Cinna, a poet

A Soothsayer (one who foretells the future)

Another Poet

Senators, Citizens, Guards, Attendants, Messengers, and **Officers**

Scene: Rome; near Sardis; near Philippi

Act 1, Scene 1

In this scene ...

A group of working class citizens who have taken a holiday join in a great parade to celebrate Caesar's military successes against Pompey's armies and to welcome him to Rome. Two tribunes, who are the elected representatives of the people, Flavius and Marullus, are angered to find these citizens participating in victory celebration for Caesar because they see the demonstration as an expression of disloyalty to Pompey.

During the encounter between the tribunes and the citizens, we learn a great deal about the political feelings in Rome in 44 B.C.E. We also learn something about the general mood of the citizens in Rome. These citizens become very significant in the development of political events as the play progresses because they illustrate the political instability and divided loyalties that run throughout the play.

3   *mechanical:* manual labourers, trades people

7   *rule:* ruler

10   *in respect of a fine workman:* in comparison with a skilled labourer

11   *cobbler:* shoemaker; also, a person who is inept at his or her work

16   *knave:* an unprincipled or crafty person

17   *be not out:* don't be angry

24   *awl:* a pointed tool used for making holes in leather

26   *trod upon neat's leather:* walked in leather shoes; *neat:* cattle

Act 1, Scene 1

Rome. A street.
Enter Flavius, Marullus, and
certain Commoners.

Flavius: Hence! Home, you idle creatures, get you home,
　Is this a holiday? what! know you not,
　Being mechanical, you ought not walk
　Upon a labouring day without the sign
　Of your profession? Speak, what trade art thou?　　　　5
First Commoner: Why, sir, a carpenter.
Marullus: Where is thy leather apron and thy rule?
　What dost thou with thy best apparel on?
　You, sir, what trade are you?
Second Commoner: Truly, sir, in respect of a fine workman,　　10
　　I am but, as you would say, a cobbler.
Marullus: But what trade art thou? answer me directly.
Second Commoner: A trade, sir, that, I hope, I may use with
　　a safe conscience; which is indeed, sir, a mender of
　　bad soles.　　　　15
Marullus: What trade, thou knave? thou naughty knave,
　　what trade?
Second Commoner: Nay, I beseech you, sir, be not out with
　　me: yet, if you be out, sir, I can mend you.
Marullus: What meanest thou by that? mend me, thou saucy
　　fellow!
Second Commoner: Why, sir, cobble you.　　　　20
Flavius: Thou art a cobbler, art thou?
Second Commoner: Truly, sir, all that I live by is with the
　　awl: I meddle with no tradesman's matters, nor women's
　　matters; but with awl. I am, indeed, sir, a surgeon to
　　old shoes; when they are in great danger, I recover　　25
　　them. As proper men as ever trod upon neat's leather
　　have gone upon my handiwork.

32	*triumph:* Caesar's return from Spain after defeating Pompey's sons
34	*tributaries:* captives
38	*Pompey:* a former ruler in Rome whom Caesar defeated in 48 B.C.E. and who was murdered a year later
47	*replication:* echo
50	*cull out:* choose to make
55	*intermit:* hold back, delay
56	*light:* fall
61	*most exalted shores:* the highest level on the shore to which the water rises
62	*basest metal:* the poor quality of their characters or dispositions
66	*decked with ceremonies:* decorated with ornaments

Flavius: But wherefore art not in thy shop to-day?
Why dost thou lead these men about the streets?
Second Commoner: Truly, sir, to wear out their shoes, to 30
get myself into more work. But, indeed, sir, we make
holiday to see Cæsar and to rejoice in his triumph.
Marullus: Wherefore rejoice? What conquest brings he home?
What tributaries follow him to Rome,
To grace in captive bonds his chariot-wheels? 35
You blocks, you stones, you worse than senseless things!
O you hard hearts, you cruel men of Rome,
Knew you not Pompey? Many a time and oft
Have you climb'd up to walls and battlements,
To towers and windows, yea, to chimney-tops, 40
Your infants in your arms, and there have sat
The live-long day, with patient expectation,
To see great Pompey pass the streets of Rome:
And when you saw his chariot but appear,
Have you not made an universal shout, 45
That Tiber trembled underneath her banks,
To hear the replication of your sounds
Made in her concave shores?
And do you now put on your best attire?
And do you now cull out a holiday? 50
And do you now strew flowers in his way
That comes in triumph over Pompey's blood?
Be gone!
Run to your houses, fall upon your knees.
Pray to the gods to intermit the plague 55
That needs must light on this ingratitude.
Flavius: Go, go, good countrymen, and, for this fault,
Assemble all the poor men of your sort;
Draw them to Tiber banks, and weep your tears
Into the channel, till the lowest stream 60
Do kiss the most exalted shores of all.
                            [*Exeunt all the Commoners.*]
See, whether their basest metal be not moved;
They vanish tongue-tied in their guiltiness.
Go you down that way towards the Capitol;
This way will I: disrobe the images, 65
If you do find them decked with ceremonies.

68   *Lupercal:* a reference to the Lupercalia, a Roman festival held on February 15 to honour Lupercus, an ancient fertility god and protector of herds and flocks

71   *the vulgar:* the common people

74   *pitch:* height
75   *else:* otherwise
76   *servile:* slavish

Marullus: May we do so?
   You know it is the feast of Lupercal.
Flavius: It is no matter; let no images
   Be hung with Cæsar's trophies. I'll about,   70
   And drive away the vulgar from the streets:
   So do you too, where you perceive them thick.
   These growing feathers plucked from Cæsar's wing
   Will make him fly an ordinary pitch,
   Who else would soar above the view of men   75
   And keep us all in servile fearfulness.

                            [Exeunt.]

Act 1, Scene 1: Activities

1. In preparation for your report to the senator for whom you work, record your observations about the encounter between the citizens and the two tribunes. How would you describe the mood of the crowd as opposed to that of the tribunes? How do you account for the differences? Share your ideas with your group before you actually write your report so that you can incorporate any additions or changes.

2. Many of the key speeches to the crowds in the play use rhetoric, which is the art of influencing the thought and conduct of the people being addressed. Marullus uses this approach in his address to the citizens (lines 33–56). In your journal, indicate how he attempts to do this. How effective is he? Share your discoveries with the group.

3. The cobbler uses many puns (plays on words so that they have two meanings) in his interchange with Flavius and Marullus. While these would have been familiar to Shakespeare's audience, many of them are puzzling to us. In your groups, paraphrase this exchange. Make a note of the unfamiliar words and references that the cobbler uses, determine how they function as puns, and note Flavius's reaction to them. Does this exchange in any way account for Marullus's sudden outburst?

   You might wish to make a collection of puns you are familiar with and include them in a dialogue you imagine you are having with another citizen while standing in the crowd.

4. Create a dialogue among members of the crowd as they disperse from the streets. Consider what they might be saying about the tribunes, about Pompey, about Caesar, and about the sudden end brought to the holiday festival. Act out your dialogue for the rest of the class.

5. Some information about Caesar's return to Rome is given to us in this scene. Note what it is and do some additional research to figure out the other historical events that occurred prior to his arrival. Present your discoveries to the class in an oral presentation using an appropriate visual form such as a chart or a map.

6. Investigate the traditions and significance of the Roman Feast of Lupercal. Why do you think Caesar chose to return to Rome at this time? What does this tell you about Caesar?

   If you had been Caesar, would you have returned at this time? Discuss your ideas.

7. Have different groups in your class create their own tableaus (freezing the action) of the scene involving the crowd and the two tribunes. Decide what mood you are trying to create and what impression you are trying to give. You may wish to have one of your class photographers record your efforts for later comparison and discussion.

For the next scene ...

Think of a situation in which you might have to choose between a loyal friend and a cause in which you sincerely believe. Discuss what you think your eventual choice would be. What consequences would you fear? Has anyone ever persuaded you to do something you later regretted? How did he or she convince you at the time?

Act 1, Scene 2

In this scene ...

Caesar's triumphal procession arrives in pomp and pageantry and soon moves on to the celebrations of the Feast of Lupercal. Cassius and Brutus, however, remain behind. They enter into a conversation about important personal and political matters that will direct the course of action for the rest of the play. Twice during their discussion we hear the crowds shouting and the trumpets blaring in the distance.

Later, Caesar and his followers return from the festivities. Speaking to Antony, Caesar expresses his personal feelings about Cassius. As the procession departs, Brutus pulls at Casca's cloak and urges Casca to report what happened at the celebrations.

Casca's account of the events leads Brutus to promise Cassius that he will think further about the matters they discussed. Alone on stage, Cassius now reveals his feelings about Brutus and his plans for his next move.

4   *run his course:* Antony, a priest of one of the orders of
        Luperci, would participate in the holy race during the
        festival.

8–9   *The barren ... sterile curse:* It was believed that women who
        could not bear children would become capable of
        pregnancy if touched by a runner during the race. As a
        conclusion to the festival of Lupercal, the priests, dressed
        in goatskins, ran about the Palatine Hill striking women with
        goatskin thongs to ensure fertility and an easy delivery.

12   *Soothsayer:* literally, "truth sayer"; a person who can see
        into the future

15   *press:* crowd

18   *Ides of March:* March 15; "Ides" means the middle of the
        month.

19   Caesar does not hear what is said and it is Brutus,
        ironically, who tells him the Soothsayer's warning.

Scene 2

A public place.

*Flourish. Enter Cæsar; Antony,
for the course; Calpurnia, Portia,
Decius, Cicero, Brutus, Cassius,
and Casca; a great crowd
following, among them a
Soothsayer.*

Cæsar: Calpurnia!
Casca: Peace, ho! Cæsar speaks.
Cæsar: Calpurnia!
Calpurnia: Here, my lord.
Cæsar: Stand you directly in Antonius' way,
    When he doth run his course. Antonius!
Antony: Cæsar, my lord?   5
Cæsar: Forget not, in your speed, Antonius,
    To touch Calpurnia; for our elders say,
    The barren, touchéd in this holy chase,
    Shake off their sterile curse.
Antony: I shall remember:
    When Cæsar says "Do this," it is performed.   10
Cæsar: Set on; and leave no ceremony out.   [*Flourish.*]
Soothsayer: Cæsar!
Cæsar: Ha! who calls?
Casca: Bid every noise be still: peace yet again!
Cæsar: Who is it in the press that calls on me?   15
    I hear a tongue, shriller than all the music,
    Cry "Cæsar!" Speak; Cæsar is turn'd to hear.
Soothsayer: Beware the Ides of March.
Cæsar: What man is that?
Brutus: A soothsayer bids you beware the Ides of March.
Cæsar: Set him before me; let me see his face.   20
Casca: Fellow, come from the throng; look upon Cæsar.

24   *Sennet:* This stage direction signals an exit or entrance and is sounded on a horn.

28   *gamesome:* fond of games

35   *bear ... hand:* treat strictly and coldly

39   *Merely:* entirely
40   *of some difference:* conflicting
41   *Conceptions ... myself:* matters or ideas that concern me alone

45   *construe:* interpret

50   *cogitations:* thoughts

58   *shadow:* reflection

Cæsar: What say'st thou to me now? speak once again.
Soothsayer: Beware the Ides of March.
Cæsar: He is a dreamer; let us leave him: pass.
     [*Sennet. Exeunt all but Brutus and Cassius.*]
Cassius: Will you go see the order of the course?   25
Brutus: Not I.
Cassius: I pray you, do.
Brutus: I am not gamesome: I do lack some part
 Of that quick spirit that is in Antony.
 Let me not hinder, Cassius, your desires;   30
 I'll leave you.
Cassius: Brutus, I do observe you now of late:
 I have not from your eyes that gentleness
 And show of love as I was wont to have:
 You bear too stubborn and too strange a hand   35
 Over your friend that loves you.
Brutus: Cassius,
 Be not deceived: if I have veil'd my look,
 I turn the trouble of my countenance
 Merely upon myself. Vexed I am
 Of late with passions of some difference,   40
 Conceptions only proper to myself,
 Which give some soil perhaps to my behaviours;
 But let not therefore my good friends be grieved—
 Among which number, Cassius, be you one—
 Nor construe any further my neglect,   45
 Than that poor Brutus, with himself at war,
 Forgets the shows of love to other men.
Cassius: Then, Brutus, I have much mistook your passion;
 By means whereof this breast of mine hath buried
 Thoughts of great value, worthy cogitations.   50
 Tell me, good Brutus, can you see your face?
Brutus: No, Cassius; for the eye sees not itself,
 But by reflection by some other things.
Cassius: 'Tis just:
 And it is very much lamented, Brutus,   55
 That you have no such mirrors as will turn
 Your hidden worthiness into your eye,
 That you might see your shadow. I have heard
 Where many of the best respect in Rome,

61   *yoke:* burden

71   *jealous on:* suspicious of
72–74   *Were I ... protester:* if I were the kind of person who gave
          my friendship and loyalty to anyone who came along

76   *scandal:* slander

78   *rout:* boisterous, common mob

80   *king:* In 510 B.C.E. the Roman people, led by an ancestor of
          Brutus, rebelled against their tyrannical king, Tarquin the
          Proud. They vowed never again to accept a king as their
          ruler and, in 509 B.C.E., established a republic—a
          government in which power is held by the people or their
          elected representatives.
85   *aught:* anything

91   *outward favour:* appearance

95   *as lief not be:* just as soon not live

Except immortal Cæsar, speaking of Brutus 60
And groaning underneath this age's yoke,
Have wish'd that noble Brutus had his eyes.
Brutus: Into what dangers would you lead me, Cassius,
That you would have me seek into myself
For that which is not in me? 65
Cassius: Therefore, good Brutus, be prepared to hear:
And since you know you cannot see yourself
So well as by reflection, I, your glass,
Will modestly discover to yourself
That of yourself which you yet know not of. 70
And be not jealous on me, gentle Brutus:
Were I a common laugher, or did use
To stale with ordinary oaths my love
To every new protester; if you know
That I do fawn on men and hug them hard 75
And after scandal them; or if you know
That I profess myself in banqueting
To all the rout, then hold me dangerous.
[Flourish and shout.]
Brutus: What means this shouting? I do fear, the people
Choose Cæsar for their king!
Cassius: Ay, do you fear it? 80
Then must I think you would not have it so.
Brutus: I would not, Cassius; yet I love him well.
But wherefore do you hold me here so long?
What is it that you would impart to me?
If it be aught toward the general good, 85
Set honour in one eye and death i' th' other,
And I will look on both indifferently:
For let the gods so speed me as I love
The name of honour more than I fear death.
Cassius: I know that virtue to be in you, Brutus, 90
As well as I do know your outward favour.
Well, honour is the subject of my story.
I cannot tell what you and other men
Think of this life; but, for my single self,
I had as lief not be as live to be 95
In awe of such a thing as I myself.
I was born free as Cæsar; so were you:

105   *Accoutred:* dressed

109   *hearts of controversy:* spirits of competition

114   *Anchises bear:* Aeneas, a Trojan, was the founder of Rome.
       When Troy was captured and burned by the Greeks,
       Aeneas escaped from the city, carrying his father Anchises
       on his back. Aeneas and his followers eventually landed in
       Italy where they ultimately founded the city of Rome.

122   *coward ... fly:* The colour faded from his lips. The wording is
       suggestive of cowardly soldiers who desert their "colours"
       or flag.
123   *bend:* look

130   *start:* control
131   *palm:* victory. A crown of palm leaves was traditionally
       given to a conqueror or victor.

136   *Colossus:* an immense statue of the god Apollo

We both have fed as well, and we can both
Endure the winter's cold as well as he:
For once, upon a raw and gusty day,   100
The troubled Tiber chafing with her shores,
Cæsar said to me, "Darest thou, Cassius, now
Leap in with me into this angry flood,
And swim to yonder point?" Upon the word,
Accoutred as I was, I plunged in   105
And bade him follow; so indeed he did.
The torrent roared, and we did buffet it
With lusty sinews, throwing it aside
And stemming it with hearts of controversy;
But ere we could arrive the point proposed,   110
Cæsar cried, "Help me, Cassius, or I sink."
I, as Æneas our great ancestor
Did from the flames of Troy upon his shoulder
The old Anchises bear, so from the waves of Tiber
Did I the tired Cæsar: and this man   115
Is now become a god, and Cassius is
A wretched creature and must bend his body
If Cæsar carelessly but nod on him.
He had a fever when he was in Spain,
And when the fit was on him, I did mark   120
How he did shake: 'tis true, this god did shake:
His coward lips did from their colour fly,
And that same eye whose bend doth awe the world
Did lose his lustre: I did hear him groan:
Ay, and that tongue of his that bade the Romans   125
Mark him and write his speeches in their books,
Alas, it cried, "Give me some drink, Titinius,"
As a sick girl. Ye gods! it doth amaze me
A man of such a feeble temper should
So get the start of the majestic world   130
And bear the palm alone.   [*Shout. Flourish.*]
Brutus: Another general shout?
  I do believe that these applauses are
  For some new honours that are heap'd on Cæsar.
Cassius: Why, man, he doth bestride the narrow world   135
  Like a Colossus, and we petty men
  Walk under his huge legs and peep about

152   *the great flood:* Cassius is referring to an old classical story in which the god Zeus destroyed the world because people had become sinful. Only two people, a husband and wife, were saved because of their virtue.

159   *a Brutus:* Lucius Junius Brutus was an ancestor of the Brutus in this play and a great leader. He led the Romans when they expelled the Tarquins from Rome, thereby establishing the Roman Republic; *brook'd:* tolerated

163   *aim:* idea

170   *meet:* appropriate
171   *chew:* think, reflect

To find ourselves dishonourable graves.
Men at some time are masters of their fates:
The fault, dear Brutus, is not in our stars,   140
But in ourselves, that we are underlings.
Brutus and Cæsar: what should be in that Cæsar?
Why should that name be sounded more than yours?
Write them together, yours is as fair a name;
Sound them, it doth become the mouth as well;   145
Weigh them, it is as heavy; conjure with 'em,
Brutus will start a spirit as soon as Cæsar.
Now, in the names of all the gods at once,
Upon what meat doth this our Cæsar feed,
That he is grown so great? Age, thou art shamed!   150
Rome, thou hast lost the breed of noble bloods!
When went there by an age, since the great flood,
But it was famed with more than with one man?
When could they say till now, that talk'd of Rome,
That her wide walls encompass'd but one man?   155
Now is it Rome indeed, and room enough,
When there is in it but one only man.
O, you and I have heard our fathers say,
There was a Brutus once that would have brook'd
The eternal devil to keep his state in Rome   160
As easily as a king.
Brutus: That you do love me, I am nothing jealous;
   What you would work me to, I have some aim:
   How I have thought of this and of these times,
   I shall recount hereafter; for this present,   165
   I would not, so with love I might entreat you,
   Be any further moved. What you have said
   I will consider; what you have to say
   I will with patience hear, and find a time
   Both meet to hear and answer such high things.   170
   Till then, my noble friend, chew upon this:
   Brutus had rather be a villager
   Than to repute himself a son of Rome
   Under these hard conditions as this time
   Is like to lay upon us.   175
Cassius: I am glad that my weak words
   Have struck but thus much show of fire from Brutus.

184   *chidden:* chided, scolded
185   *Cicero:* an influential senator and speaker, often in open opposition to both Caesar and Mark Antony
186   *ferret:* a small animal with red eyes
188   *cross'd in conference:* challenged or contradicted in debate

197   *well given:* a supporter (of Caesar's)

202–203   *he looks ... men:* He sees through people's actions to their motives.

213   *deaf:* Historically there is no evidence that Caesar was deaf. The notion of deafness is possibly an invention of Shakespeare's, perhaps derived from stories he heard, or maybe included as a dramatic device.

Brutus: The games are done and Cæsar is returning.
Cassius: As they pass by, pluck Casca by the sleeve;
    And he will, after his sour fashion, tell you 180
    What hath proceeded worthy note to-day.

[*Re-enter Cæsar and his train.*]

Brutus: I will do so. But, look you, Cassius,
    The angry spot doth glow on Cæsar's brow,
    And all the rest look like a chidden train:
    Calpurnia's cheek is pale; and Cicero 185
    Looks with such ferret and such fiery eyes
    As we have seen him in the Capitol,
    Being cross'd in conference by some senators.
Cassius: Casca will tell us what the matter is.
Cæsar: Antonius! 190
Antony: Cæsar?
Cæsar: Let me have men about me that are fat,
    Sleek-headed men, and such as sleep o'-nights:
    Yond Cassius has a lean and hungry look;
    He thinks too much: such men are dangerous. 195
Antony: Fear him not, Cæsar; he's not dangerous;
    He is a noble Roman and well given.
Cæsar: Would he were fatter. But I fear him not:
    Yet if my name were liable to fear,
    I do not know the man I should avoid 200
    So soon as that spare Cassius. He reads much;
    He is a great observer, and he looks
    Quite through the deeds of men; he loves no plays,
    As thou dost, Antony; he hears no music;
    Seldom he smiles, and smiles in such a sort 205
    As if he mock'd himself and scorn'd his spirit
    That could be moved to smile at anything.
    Such men as he be never at heart's ease
    While they behold a greater than themselves,
    And therefore are they very dangerous. 210
    I rather tell thee what is to be fear'd
    Than what I fear; for always I am Cæsar.
    Come on my right hand, for this ear is deaf,
    And tell me truly what thou think'st of him.
        [*Sennet. Exeunt Cæsar and his train. Casca remains.*]

216   *chanced:* happened

228   *marry:* truly (a mild oath, from "By the Virgin Mary")

235   *mark:* pay attention to

237   *coronets:* small crowns

243   *rabblement:* rabble, mob
244   *chopt:* chapped, rough

247   *swounded:* fainted

250   *But, soft:* Wait a minute.

253   *falling sickness:* epilepsy, a brain disorder characterized by seizures and usually a loss of consciousness; thus, people literally fall to the ground.

Casca: You pulled me by the cloak; would you speak with
    me?   215

Brutus: Ay, Casca; tell us what hath chanced to-day,
   That Cæsar looks so sad.

Casca: Why, you were with him, were you not?

Brutus: I should not then ask Casca what had chanced.

Casca: Why, there was a crown offered him: and being   220
    offered him, he put it by with the back of his hand,
    thus; and then the people fell a-shouting.

Brutus: What was the second noise for?

Casca: Why, for that too.

Cassius: They shouted thrice; what was the last cry for?   225

Casca: Why, for that too.

Brutus: Was the crown offered him thrice?

Casca: Ay, marry, was't, and he put it by thrice, every time
    gentler than other; and at every putting by mine
    honest neighbours shouted.   230

Cassius: Who offered him the crown?

Casca: Why, Antony.

Brutus: Tell us the manner of it, gentle Casca.

Casca: I can as well be hanged as tell the manner of it: it
    was mere foolery; I did not mark it. I saw Mark Antony 235
    offer him a crown; yet 'twas not a crown neither, 'twas
    one of these coronets; and, as I told you, he put it by
    once: but, for all that, to my thinking, he would fain
    have had it. Then he offered it to him again; then
    he put it by again: but, to my thinking, he was very   240
    loath to lay his fingers off it. And then he offered it
    the third time; he put it the third time by: and still as
    he refused it, the rabblement hooted and clapped their
    chopt hands and threw up their sweaty nightcaps, and
    uttered such a deal of stinking breath because Cæsar   245
    refused the crown, that it had almost choked Cæsar; for
    he swounded and fell down at it: and for mine own
    part, I durst not laugh, for fear of opening my lips and
    receiving the bad air.

Cassius: But, soft, I pray you: what, did Cæsar swound?   250

Casca: He fell down in the market-place, and foamed at
    mouth, and was speechless.

Brutus: 'Tis very like: he hath the falling sickness.

269   *amiss:* improper

272   *heed:* notice

280   *and:* if

285   *put to silence:* It is unclear whether this is to be taken
        literally or whether we should infer that the two tribunes
        were stripped of their offices, thereby effectively "put to
        silence."

Cassius: No, Cæsar hath it not; but you and I
  And honest Casca, we have the falling sickness. 255
Casca: I know not what you mean by that; but, I am sure,
  Cæsar fell down. If the tag-rag people did not clap him
  and hiss him, according as he pleased and displeased
  them, as they use to do the players in the theatre,
  I am no true man. 260
Brutus: What said he when he came unto himself?
Casca: Marry, before he fell down, when he perceived the
  common herd was glad he refused the crown, he
  plucked me ope his doublet and offered them his throat
  to cut. An I had been a man of any occupation, if I 265
  would not have taken him at a word, I would I might
  go to hell among the rogues. And so he fell. When
  he came to himself again, he said, if he had done or said
  any thing amiss, he desired their worships to think it
  was his infirmity. Three or four wenches, where I stood, 270
  cried, "Alas, good soul!" and forgave him with all their
  hearts: but there's no heed to be taken of them; if Cæsar
  had stabbed their mothers, they would have done
  no less.
Brutus: And after that, he came, thus sad, away? 275
Casca: Ay.
Cassius: Did Cicero say anything?
Casca: Ay, he spoke Greek.
Cassius: To what effect?
Casca: Nay, and I tell you that, I'll ne'er look you i' th' 280
  face again: but those that understood him smiled at one
  another and shook their heads; but, for mine own
  part, it was Greek to me. I could tell you more news
  too: Marullus and Flavius, for pulling scarfs off
  Cæsar's images, are put to silence. Fare you well. 285
  There was more foolery yet, if I could remember it.
Cassius: Will you sup with me to-night, Casca?
Casca: No, I am promised forth.
Cassius: Will you dine with me to-morrow?
Casca: Ay, if I be alive and your mind hold and your dinner 290
  worth the eating.
Cassius: Good: I will expect you.
Casca: Do so. Farewell both. [*Exit.*]

295   *quick mettle:* full of spirit and enthusiasm

298   *tardy form:* appearance of being slow-witted

299   *This rudeness ... wit:* His pretence of being stupid emphasizes his intelligence.

308–309   *Thy honourable metal ... it is disposed:* Cassius believes Brutus's honourable character can be changed (*wrought:* crafted, shaped) from its normal state.

312   *bear me hard:* dislikes me

315   *several hands:* different handwritings

320   *seat him sure:* make his position secure, be careful

Brutus: What a blunt fellow is this grown to be!
   He was quick mettle when he went to school.   295
Cassius: So is he now in execution
   Of any bold or noble enterprise,
   However he puts on this tardy form.
   This rudeness is a sauce to his good wit,
   Which gives men stomach to digest his words   300
   With better appetite.
Brutus: And so it is. For this time I will leave you:
   To-morrow, if you please to speak with me,
   I will come home to you; or, if you will,
   Come home to me, and I will wait for you.   305
Cassius: I will do so: till then, think of the world.
                            [*Exit Brutus.*]
   Well, Brutus, thou art noble; yet, I see,
   Thy honourable metal may be wrought
   From that it is disposed: therefore it is meet
   That noble minds keep ever with their likes;   310
   For who so firm that cannot be seduced?
   Cæsar doth bear me hard; but he loves Brutus:
   If I were Brutus now and he were Cassius,
   He should not humour me. I will this night,
   In several hands, in at his windows throw,   315
   As if they came from several citizens
   Writings all tending to the great opinion
   That Rome holds of his name; wherein obscurely
   Cæsar's ambition should be glanced at:
   And after this let Cæsar seat him sure;   320
   For we will shake him, or worse days endure.
                                [*Exit.*]

Act 1, Scene 2: Activities

1. You have just had an opportunity to interview Julius Caesar on TV. You have been told to write a news release about him, based on your interview, revealing details that you could not elicit on TV. How do you do that? Can you really reveal things that were noted "off the record"? What do you put in your news release? Write it so you don't get sued.

2. Casca and Cassius meet for dinner the next day in a Roman restaurant. Record their conversation. What will you do with this information and whom will you tell?

3. Cassius talks about sending letters to Brutus to be delivered on the day of the procession. Write one of them and be convincing but careful in case it doesn't reach Brutus but falls into another's hands. If you are caught, you are in dire Roman trouble.

   Caesar says that Cassius has a "lean and hungry look." What do you think this metaphor means? Possibly, there are persons you have encountered in your life, have read about in magazines, or have seen interviewed on TV that could fit this description. In your journal, record your impressions of anyone who comes to your mind. Insert this individual into the play where you think he or she might probably fit, giving them only *one* line of dialogue. What would this person say?

4. Often politicians are depicted as having two faces or personalities—a public one and a private one. Create a cover for a news magazine in which you depict your version of Cassius or Brutus or Caesar in both of these modes. Explain why you have chosen your portrayal.

5. A soliloquy is a speech delivered by a character who is talking to himself or herself while alone or while ignoring any other characters present. In your journal, decide how you interpret the difference between the Cassius we see in conversation with others in the play and the Cassius who

speaks in the soliloquy at the end of the scene. What conclusions do you draw from your observations? Share these observations with your class or with your group.

6. Discuss your impressions of Cassius with a partner using evidence from the scene to support your opinion. Create a profile of Cassius in your journal. As you continue to explore the play, add to your profile of Cassius. Decide whether the new information you gain changes your opinion of him.

7. Imagine you are Cassius and you are riding a subway or a bus to work and thinking about your part in the day's events. Explain to yourself what prompted your soliloquy (lines 307–321). As Cassius, you keep a daily journal. What do you record in that journal after this particular ride is over and you have had time to reflect on what you were thinking about? Do you want to share this journal entry? If you do, with whom would you share it?

8. You are Julius Caesar, a prominent public figure. You have been warned that something nasty might happen to you. You keep a diary. What do you write in it after you have heard the Soothsayer's words?

For the next scene ...

There are people who believe that certain signs occur that predict upcoming events (omens). In your journal, record where you stand on this issue. Have you, or has someone you know, ever had an experience that seems unexplainable? What is your opinion about what are often called paranormal experiences?

Act 1, Scene 3

In this scene ...

A month has passed. It is March 14 and a terrific storm is battering Rome with all the pyrotechnics that violent storms bring. Casca is petrified of it and recounts a series of bizarre events he claims to have witnessed. Cicero is equally amazed at the strange sights that have occurred. Cassius arrives and uses the storm and the superstitions that Casca and Cicero hold to advance his plans to have the two join in the plot to overthrow Caesar. Cassius is concerned that Caesar will be crowned as the supreme leader and head of state in Rome and wants to prevent that possibility at all costs. In this scene the conspiracy against Caesar begins in earnest.

3–4   *sway of earth ... unfirm:* It was believed that the earth was anchored in the universe and immovable, and everything else revolved around it.

5   *scolding:* violently blasting or raging
6   *rived:* split

19   *put up:* put away
20   *Against the Capitol:* close to the Senate

26   *bird of night:* owl

28   *prodigies:* unnatural events

Scene 3

Rome. A street.

*Thunder and lightning. Enter, from
opposite sides, Casca, with his
sword drawn, and Cicero.*

Cicero: Good even, Casca: brought you Cæsar home?
  Why are you breathless? And why stare you so?
Casca: Are not you moved, when all the sway of earth
  Shakes like a thing unfirm? O Cicero,
  I have seen tempests, when the scolding winds   5
  Have rived the knotty oaks, and I have seen
  The ambitious ocean swell and rage and foam,
  To be exalted with the threatening clouds:
  But never till to-night, never till now,
  Did I go through a tempest dropping fire.   10
  Either there is a civil strife in heaven,
  Or else the world, too saucy with the gods,
  Incenses them to send destruction.
Cicero: Why, saw you anything more wonderful?
Casca: A common slave, you know him well by sight,   15
  Held up his left hand, which did flame and burn
  Like twenty torches join'd, and yet his hand,
  Not sensible of fire, remained unscorch'd.
  Besides—I ha' not since put up my sword—
  Against the Capitol I met a lion,   20
  Who glared upon me, and went surly by
  Without annoying me: and there were drawn
  Upon a heap a hundred ghastly women
  Transformed with their fear, who swore they saw
  Men all in fire walk up and down the streets.   25
  And yesterday the bird of night did sit
  Even at noon-day upon the market-place,
  Hooting and shrieking. When these prodigies

29   *conjointly meet:* coincide

31   *portentous:* foreboding, threatening

35   *clean from:* separate or apart from

48   *unbraced:* with shirt unfastened
49   *thunder-stone:* what we would understand as a clap of
        thunder and identify as lightning; it was believed at the time
        that flaming stones actually fell from the sky during severe
        storms.

56   *heralds:* omens

58   *want:* lack

Do so conjointly meet, let not men say
"These are their reasons: they are natural";   30
For, I believe, they are portentous things
Unto the climate that they point upon.
Cicero: Indeed, it is a strange-disposed time:
But men may construe things after their fashion,
Clean from the purpose of the things themselves.   35
Comes Cæsar to the Capitol to-morrow?
Casca: He doth; for he did bid Antonius
Send word to you he would be there to-morrow.
Cicero: Good-night, then, Casca; this disturbed sky
Is not to walk in.
Casca: Farewell, Cicero.   *[Exit Cicero.]*   40

[*Enter Cassius.*]

Cassius: Who's there?
Casca: A Roman.
Cassius: Casca, by your voice.
Casca: Your ear is good, Cassius, what night is this!
Cassius: A very pleasing night to honest men.
Casca: Who ever knew the heavens menace so?
Cassius: Those that have known the earth so full of faults.   45
For my part, I have walk'd about the streets,
Submitting me unto the perilous night,
And thus unbraced, Casca, as you see,
Have bared my bosom to the thunder-stone;
And when the cross blue lightning seem'd to open   50
The breast of heaven, I did present myself
Even in the aim and very flash of it.
Casca: But wherefore did you so much tempt the heavens?
It is the part of men to fear and tremble,
When the most mighty gods by tokens send   55
Such dreadful heralds to astonish us.
Cassius: You are dull, Casca, and those sparks of life
That should be in a Roman you do want,
Or else you use not. You look pale and gaze
And put on fear and cast yourself in wonder,   60
To see the strange impatience of the heavens:
But if you would consider the true cause
Why all these fires, why all these gliding ghosts,

64   *from quality and kind:* against their natures

66   *ordinance:* natural ways of behaving

77   *prodigious:* threatening
78   *fearful:* inspiring fear in others

81   *thews:* sinews, muscles

84   *yoke and sufferance:* endurance of this burden; that is, to agree to suffer under Caesar's rule

91   *therein:* a reference to the dagger

95   *be retentive to:* hold in

101   *bondman:* slave

Why birds and beasts from quality and kind,
Why old men fool and children calculate, 65
Why all these things change from their ordinance
Their natures and preformed faculties,
To monstrous quality, why, you shall find
That heaven hath infused them with these spirits,
To make them instruments of fear and warning 70
Unto some monstrous state.
Now could I, Casca, name to thee a man
Most like this dreadful night,
That thunders, lightens, opens graves, and roars
As doth the lion in the Capitol, 75
A man no mightier than thyself or me
In personal action, yet prodigious grown
And fearful, as these strange eruptions are.
Casca: 'Tis Cæsar that you mean; is it not, Cassius?
Cassius: Let it be who it is: for Romans now 80
Have thews and limbs like to their ancestors;
But, woe the while! our fathers' minds are dead,
And we are govern'd with our mothers' spirits;
Our yoke and sufferance show us womanish.
Casca: Indeed, they say the senators to-morrow 85
Mean to establish Cæsar as a king;
And he shall wear his crown by sea and land,
In every place, save here in Italy.
Cassius: I know where I will wear this dagger then:
Cassius from bondage will deliver Cassius: 90
Therein, ye gods, you make the weak most strong;
Therein, ye gods, you tyrants do defeat:
Nor stony tower, nor walls of beaten brass,
Nor airless dungeon, nor strong links of iron,
Can be retentive to the strength of spirit; 95
But life, being weary of these worldly bars,
Never lacks power to dismiss itself.
If I know this, know all the world besides,
That part of tyranny that I do bear
I can shake off at pleasure. [*Thunder still.*]
Casca: So can I: 100
So every bondman in his own hand bears
The power to cancel his captivity.

106 *hinds:* female deer

109 *offal:* waste, garbage

114 *My answer must be made:* My response must be given, assuming that Casca is not to be trusted.

117 *fleering:* sneering, scornful
118 *Be factious for redress:* form a group to challenge or correct

125 *by this they stay:* by now they are waiting
126 *Pompey's porch:* an open park-like area in front of the theatre built by Pompey
128–130 *And the complexion ... most terrible:* What is happening in the storm outside is as violent as the plot we are planning.

135–136 *incorporate to our attempts:* joining us in the conspiracy
136, 139 *Am I not stay'd for?:* "Isn't someone waiting for me?" (a possible reference to his co-conspirators)

Cassius: And why should Cæsar be a tyrant then?
  Poor man! I know he would not be a wolf,
  But that he sees the Romans are but sheep: 105
  He were no lion, were not Romans hinds.
  Those that with haste will make a mighty fire
  Begin it with weak straws: what trash is Rome,
  What rubbish and what offal, when it serves
  For the base matter to illuminate   110
  So vile a thing as Cæsar! But, O grief,
  Where hast thou led me? I perhaps speak this
  Before a willing bondman; then I know
  My answer must be made. But I am arm'd,
  And dangers are to me indifferent.   115
Casca: You speak to Casca, and to such a man
  That is no fleering tell-tale. Hold, my hand:
  Be factious for redress of all these griefs,
  And I will set this foot of mine as far
  As who goes farthest.
Cassius: There's a bargain made.   120
  Now know you, Casca, I have moved already
  Some certain of the noblest-minded Romans
  To undergo with me an enterprise
  Of honourable-dangerous consequence;
  And I do know, by this they stay for me   125
  In Pompey's porch: for now, this fearful night,
  There is no stir or walking in the streets;
  And the complexion of the element
  Is feverous like the work we have in hand,
  Most bloody-fiery, and most terrible.   130

  [*Enter Cinna.*]

Casca: Stand close awhile, for here comes one in haste.
Cassius: 'Tis Cinna; I do know him by his gait;
  He is a friend. Cinna, where haste you so?
Cinna: To find out you. Who's that? Metellus Cimber?
Cassius: No, it is Casca; one incorporate   135
  To our attempts. Am I not stay'd for, Cinna?
Cinna: I am glad on't. What a fearful night is this!
  There's two or three of us have seen strange sights.
Cassius: Am I not stay'd for? tell me.

143   *praetor's chair:* the official chair in which Brutus sits as a magistrate, a position just below that of consul; a consul was a chief magistrate of the Roman Republic. At this time, Caesar and Anthony were consuls but Brutus wasn't.

145   *set this up with wax:* seal

150   *hie:* hurry

153   *ere:* before

159   *countenance:* support; Casca means both support and demeanour or appearance; *alchemy:* early science of chemistry, especially the attempts to change common metals such as lead and tin into gold

162   *conceited:* understood

Cinna: Yes, you are.
   O Cassius, if you could   140
   But win the noble Brutus to our party——
Cassius: Be you content: good Cinna, take this paper,
   And look you lay it in the prætor's chair,
   Where Brutus may but find it; and throw this
   In at his window; set this up with wax   145
   Upon old Brutus' statue: all this done,
   Repair to Pompey's porch, where you shall find us.
   Is Decius Brutus and Trebonius there?
Cinna: All but Metellus Cimber; and he's gone
   To seek you at your house. Well, I will hie,   150
   And so bestow these papers as you bade me.
Cassius: That done, repair to Pompey's theatre.
                                    [Exit Cinna.]
   Come, Casca, you and I will yet ere day
   See Brutus at his house: three parts of him
   Is ours already, and the man entire   155
   Upon the next encounter yields him ours.
Casca: O, he sits high in all the people's hearts:
   And that which would appear offence in us,
   His countenance, like richest alchemy,
   Will change to virtue and to worthiness.   160
Cassius: Him and his worth and our great need of him
   You have right well conceited. Let us go,
   For it is after midnight, and ere day
   We will awake him and be sure of him.   *[Exeunt.]*

Act 1, Scene 3: Activities

1. As an Elizabethan director, explain how you would create the storm effects in this play, given that it was performed in the middle of the day. Describe the relationship between the weather and the events taking place. Can you think of a story, TV show, or movie in which the weather played this type of role?

   You will probably want to make your own sound track to reinforce your concept and explain why you have chosen your approach. Present this to the class.

2. Let us assume that Cassius is a man with a purpose and he is thinking about what he just said (lines 45–130). Create a soliloquy for him that might reveal his true motivations.

3. Having children is a big issue for some of the characters in this play. Write a short essay explaining why this is so important in terms of what other things are going on.

4. There are many political events happening today that resemble those you have encountered in the play so far. Give a description of one event that has engaged you and relate it to the play. You can use this as a journal entry or as an article for publication in a local newspaper.

Act 1: Consider the Whole Act

1. We have no way of knowing what Shakespeare thought, but it has been proposed that Brutus was a follower of Stoicism, a belief that the mind should rule the body and that anything physical should be ignored. Stoics believed that all real or material things, such as humans and the planets, were ruled by the same universal force. In a 500-word essay, explore this issue from Brutus's point of view. Of course, you must do some research on the topic of Stoicism before making your presentation. When you feel ready, present your findings to the class as a whole.

2. The opposite to Stoicism is the Epicurean philosophy. It proposes that there is no connection at all between human beings and the revolutions of the planets. While Stoics seem to believe that the emotions are harmful and people should be indifferent to either pleasure or pain, the Epicureans believed just the opposite: that the "real" life is the sensual life. They believed that horoscopes were essentially bogus. The Epicurean philosophy also suggests that if we find ourselves oppressed and in difficulty, then it is our own fault for not taking action to prevent whatever it was that we didn't want to happen.

   Cassius is considered to hold the Epicurean point of view. What do you think? Is there any evidence in the play to support this theory? Record your thoughts in your journal, which may well be personal, but be prepared to share some of what you have written with the rest of the class.

3. You are a newscaster interviewing Caesar. You don't particularly like what he is doing, but the network has scheduled a national TV interview with you as host. What questions are you going to ask him? Record your interview on tape or in written form, or both. Decide before the interview, as a Roman citizen, whether you are simply a loyal follower, someone who agrees with whatever a leader says, or someone who has an individual perspective on what is going on. Answers to these questions will help you

to determine the direction your interview will take. Present your interview to the class.

4. There are a number of personality clashes evident in this act. Discuss these in your group and determine what *three* of the major issues of disagreement might be. Prepare a solution to these problems, looking at them as if they were issues to be dealt with today. How do you deal with the persons who think they have lost the argument? You can be Cassius, Brutus, Caesar, or a member of the crowd. What happens if there is no resolution?

5. One of the clever devices in Elizabethan drama is the use of language to compensate for the lack of concrete visuals of the kind we would normally expect in a filmed version. Look back on this scene and figure out how language is used to create vivid visual images. You are now a director and have made notes about your observations. You are going to film this act. Record how you will do it.

6. Cassius makes a great point about "seducing" Brutus in his soliloquy (Scene 2, lines 307–321), and we learn a great deal about him from what he says. What does "seducing" really mean? How can one person actually "seduce" another? Solve these problems in your groups and then individually draw a picture of Cassius talking to Brutus. If Cassius could be called "The Seducer," how do you show this characteristic in your drawing (see line 311)? You don't have to be an artist to try this; just trust yourself and your interpretation of the text so far. Once you are finished, you could arrange a class picture display to see the differences in interpretation.

For the next scene ...

Think of a time when you were faced with a serious problem that required you to make an important decision. What did you do? How did you feel?

Act 2, Scene 1

In this scene ...

It is early in the morning of the Ides of March, and Brutus is in his orchard. As the thunder still sounds in the distance and the last flashes of lightning illumine the dark sky, we learn about the storm that is raging within Brutus. He has made his decision and attempts to justify it by giving his reasons. Soon the conspirators arrive and final plans for the assassination of Caesar are discussed and arranged. When Brutus is once again alone, his wife Portia enters. She urges him to share with her what is troubling him. Their conversation is interrupted by the arrival of the ailing Ligarius, who pledges his loyalty to Brutus. The two men then leave together for Caesar's house.

11	*spurn at:* reject, repel
12	*general:* the public welfare

19	*Remorse:* mercy, compassion
20	*affections:* emotions

24	*round:* rung (of a ladder)
28	*lest ... prevent:* Caesar may become too powerful and turn his back on his supporters. To prevent this, we must stop him now.
28–29	*the quarrel ... he is:* There is no reason or cause to complain about what he is now.

Act 2, Scene 1

Rome. Brutus' orchard.

Enter Brutus.

Brutus: What, Lucius, ho!
  I cannot, by the progress of the stars,
  Give guess how near to day. Lucius, I say!
  I would it were my fault to sleep so soundly.
  When, Lucius, when? awake, I say! what, Lucius!   5

[*Enter Lucius.*]

Lucius: Call'd you, my lord?
Brutus: Get me a taper in my study, Lucius:
  When it is lighted, come and call me here.
Lucius: I will, my lord.   [*Exit.*]
Brutus: It must be by his death: and, for my part,   10
  I know no personal cause to spurn at him,
  But for the general. He would be crown'd:
  How that might change his nature, there's the question.
  It is the bright day that brings forth the adder;
  And that craves wary walking. Crown him?—that;—   15
  And then, I grant, we put a sting in him,
  That at his will he may do danger with.
  The abuse of greatness is when it disjoins
  Remorse from power: and, to speak truth of Cæsar,
  I have not known when his affections sway'd   20
  More than his reason. But 'tis a common proof,
  That lowliness is young ambition's ladder,
  Whereto the climber-upward turns his face;
  But when he once attains the upmost round,
  He then unto the ladder turns his back,   25
  Looks in the clouds, scorning the base degrees
  By which he did ascend: so Cæsar may;
  Then, lest he may, prevent. And, since the quarrel

30   *augmented:* increased, enlarged

44   *exhalations:* meteors

47   *redress:* remedy, set right

52   *under one man's awe:* in respect and fear of one man

58   *Thy full petition:* all you have asked for

Will bear no colour for the thing he is,
Fashion it thus; that what he is, augmented,   30
Would run to these and these extremities:
And therefore think him as a serpent's egg
Which, hatch'd, would, as his kind, grow mischievous,
And kill him in the shell.

[*Re-enter Lucius.*]

Lucius: The taper burneth in your closet, sir.   35
Searching the window for a flint I found
This paper thus seal'd up, and I am sure
It did not lie there when I went to bed.
                                        [*Gives him the letter.*]
Brutus: Get you to bed again; it is not day.
Is not to-morrow, boy, the Ides of March?   40
Lucius: I know not, sir.
Brutus: Look in the calendar, and bring me word.
Lucius: I will, sir.   [*Exit.*]
Brutus: The exhalations whizzing in the air
Give so much light that I may read by them.   45
                                        [*Opens the letter and reads.*]
    "Brutus, thou sleep'st: awake and see thyself.
    Shall Rome, etc. Speak, strike, redress!
    Brutus, thou sleep'st: awake!"
Such instigations have been often dropp'd
Where I have took them up.   50
"Shall Rome, etc." Thus must I piece it out:
Shall Rome stand under one man's awe? What, Rome?
My ancestors did from the streets of Rome
The Tarquin drive, when he was call'd a king.
"Speak, strike, redress!" Am I entreated   55
To speak and strike? O Rome, I make thee promise,
If the redress will follow, thou receivest
Thy full petition at the hand of Brutus!

[*Re-enter Lucius.*]

Lucius: Sir, March is wasted fourteen days.
                                        [*Knocking within.*]
Brutus: 'Tis good. Go to the gate; somebody knocks.   60
                                        [*Exit Lucius.*]

65   *phantasma:* hallucination

66   *The Genius ... instruments:* An immortal spirit or angel
(genius) was thought to rule people through the use of
mortal faculties (bodily powers that included the emotions,
the will, and the ability to reason).

67   *in council:* at war. Brutus is suggesting that he is in conflict
with the immortal spirit that decides what will happen.

70   *brother:* Cassius is married to Brutus's sister; therefore, they
are brothers-in-law.

73   *hats:* It is doubtful that Romans wore hats, although the
actors in Shakespeare's production probably did.

76   *mark of favour:* distinguishing features

82   *affability:* friendliness

83   *for if ... on:* if you walk showing your true appearance

84–85   *Not Erebus ... from prevention:* In Greek mythology Erebus
was the dark region underneath the earth through which the
dead passed on their way to Hades, the underworld. Brutus
is saying that if conspiracy were not masked by a friendly
appearance and manner, there would be no place dark
enough to hide a face of such evil.

Since Cassius first did whet me against Cæsar,
I have not slept.
Between the acting of a dreadful thing
And the first motion, all the interim is
Like a phantasma or a hideous dream: 65
The Genius and the mortal instruments
Are then in council; and the state of man,
Like to a little kingdom, suffers then
The nature of an insurrection.

[*Re-enter Lucius*]

Lucius: Sir, 'tis your brother Cassius at the door,   70
    Who doth desire to see you.
Brutus: Is he alone?
Lucius: No, sir, there are more with him.
Brutus: Do you know them?
Lucius: No, sir; their hats are pluck'd about their ears,
    And half their faces buried in their cloaks,
    That by no means I may discover them   75
    By any mark of favour.
Brutus: Let 'em enter.   [*Exit Lucius.*]
    They are the faction. O conspiracy,
    Shamest thou to show thy dangerous brow by night,
    When evils are most free? O, then, by day
    Where wilt thou find a cavern dark enough   80
    To mask thy monstrous visage? Seek none, conspiracy;
    Hide it in smiles and affability:
    For if thou path, thy native semblance on,
    Not Erebus itself were dim enough
    To hide thee from prevention.   85

[*Enter the Conspirators, Cassius, Casca, Decius, Cinna,*
    Metellus Cimber, and Trebonius.]

Cassius: I think we are too bold upon your rest:
    Good-morrow, Brutus; do we trouble you?
Brutus: I have been up this hour, awake all night.
    Know I these men that come along with you?
Cassius: Yes, every man of them: and no man here   90
    But honours you; and every one doth wish
    You had but that opinion of yourself

104   *fret:* streak across

115   *sufferance:* endurance

118   *high-sighted:* arrogant

126   *palter:* hesitate

129   *cautelous:* deceitful
130   *carrions:* dead, rotting corpses

Which every noble Roman bears of you.
This is Trebonius.
Brutus: He is welcome hither.
Cassius: This, Decius Brutus.
Brutus: He is welcome too.   95
Cassius: This, Casca; this, Cinna; and this, Metellus Cimber.
Brutus: They are all welcome.
    What watchful cares do interpose themselves
    Betwixt your eyes and night?
Cassius: Shall I entreat a word?   [*They whisper.*]   100
Decius: Here lies the east: doth not the day break here?
Casca: No.
Cinna: O, pardon, sir, it doth; and yon grey lines
    That fret the clouds are messengers of day.
Casca: You shall confess that you are both deceived.   105
    Here, as I point my sword, the sun arises;
    Which is a great way growing on the south,
    Weighing the youthful season of the year.
    Some two months hence up higher toward the north
    He first presents his fire; and the high east   110
    Stands, as the Capitol, directly here.
Brutus: Give me your hands all over, one by one.
Cassius: And let us swear our resolution.
Brutus: No, not an oath: if not the face of men,
    The sufferance of our souls, the time's abuse,—   115
    If these be motives weak, break off betimes,
    And every man hence to his idle bed;
    So let high-sighted tyranny range on,
    Till each man drop by lottery. But if these,
    As I am sure they do, bear fire enough   120
    To kindle cowards and to steel with valour
    The melting spirits of women, then, countrymen,
    What need we any spur but our own cause
    To prick us to redress? what other bond
    Than secret Romans, that have spoke the word,   125
    And will not palter? and what other oath
    Than honesty to honesty engaged
    That this shall be, or we will fall for it?
    Swear priests and cowards and men cautelous,
    Old feeble carrions and such suffering souls   130

138   *of a several bastardy:* not being pure Roman blood; that is, not being of true Roman spirit and character

150   *break with:* confide in

155   *urged:* suggested

160   *annoy:* harm

164   *envy:* malice

That welcome wrongs; unto bad causes swear
Such creatures as men doubt; but do not stain
The even virtue of our enterprise,
Nor the insuppressive mettle of our spirits,
To think that or our cause or our performance   135
Did need an oath; when every drop of blood
That every Roman bears, and nobly bears,
Is guilty of a several bastardy,
If he do break the smallest particle
Of any promise that hath pass'd from him.   140
Cassius: But what of Cicero? shall we sound him?
   I think he will stand very strong with us.
Casca: Let us not leave him out.
Cinna: No, by no means.
Metellus: O, let us have him, for his silver hairs
   Will purchase us a good opinion,   145
   And buy men's voices to commend our deeds:
   It shall be said, his judgment ruled our hands;
   Our youths and wildness shall no whit appear,
   But all be buried in his gravity.
Brutus: O, name him not: let us not break with him: 150
   For he will never follow anything
   That other men begin.
Cassius: Then leave him out.
Casca: Indeed he is not fit.
Decius: Shall no man else be touch'd but only Cæsar?
Cassius: Decius, well urged: I think it is not meet,   155
   Mark Antony, so well beloved of Cæsar,
   Should outlive Cæsar: we shall find of him
   A shrewd contriver; and you know, his means,
   If he improve them, may well stretch so far
   As to annoy us all: which to prevent,   160
   Let Antony and Cæsar fall together.
Brutus: Our course will seem too bloody, Caius Cassius,
   To cut the head off and then hack the limbs,
   Like wrath in death and envy afterwards;
   For Antony is but a limb of Cæsar: 165
   Let us be sacrificers, but not butchers, Caius.
   We all stand up against the spirit of Cæsar;
   And in the spirit of men there is no blood:

175   *subtle:* crafty

179   *common eyes:* the general public
180   *purgers:* healers, cleansers

184   *ingrafted:* strongly rooted

188   *that were much:* that would be difficult for him to do

191   *Clock strikes:* (stage direction) Striking clocks were not
       actually invented until the thirteenth century.

196   *Quite from the main opinion:* very different from the strong
       opinion
197   *ceremonies:* religious practices that predict the future
198   *prodigies:* signs of disaster
200   *augurers:* a group of religious officials who foretold the
       future from omens

O, that we then could come by Cæsar's spirit,
And not dismember Cæsar! But, alas!   170
Cæsar must bleed for it! And, gentle friends.
Let's kill him boldly, but not wrathfully;
Let's carve him as a dish fit for the gods,
Not hew him as a carcase fit for hounds:
And let our hearts, as subtle masters do,   175
Stir up their servants to an act of rage,
And after seem to chide 'em. This shall make
Our purpose necessary and not envious:
Which so appearing to the common eyes,
We shall be call'd purgers, not murderers.   180
And for Mark Antony, think not of him;
For he can do no more than Cæsar's arm
When Cæsar's head is off.
Cassius: Yet I fear him;
  For in the ingrafted love he bears to Cæsar——
Brutus: Alas! good Cassius, do not think of him.   185
  If he love Cæsar, all that he can do
  Is to himself, take thought and die for Cæsar:
  And that were much he should, for he is given
  To sports, to wildness, and much company.
Trebonius: There is no fear in him; let him not die;   190
  For he will live, and laugh at this hereafter.
                                        [*Clock strikes.*]
Brutus: Peace! count the clock.
Cassius: The clock hath stricken three.
Trebonius: 'Tis time to part.
Cassius: But it is doubtful yet
  Whether Cæsar will come forth to-day, or no;
  For he is superstitious grown of late,   195
  Quite from the main opinion he held once
  Of fantasy, of dreams and ceremonies:
  It may be, these apparent prodigies,
  The unaccustom'd terror of this night,
  And the persuasion of his augurers,   200
  May hold him from the Capitol to-day.
Decius: Never fear that: if he be so resolved,
  I can o'ersway him; for he loves to hear
  That unicorns may be betray'd with trees,

204–206 *That unicorns ... toils:* It was believed that a hunter should stand behind a tree to catch a unicorn. When the unicorn charged, it would drive its horn into the tree and be captured. It was also thought that a bear would be so occupied with gazing at its reflection in a mirror that a hunter could catch it easily. Elephants were caught in holes lightly covered with branches and lions were caught by hidden snares.

210 *bent:* direction

213 *uttermost:* latest

215 *bear Caesar hard:* holds a grudge against Caesar

216 *rated:* scolded

220 *fashion him:* shape him to our purposes; persuade him to become a member of our conspiracy

225 *put on:* display, reveal

231 *no figures nor no fantasies:* no problems or imaginings

And bears with glasses, elephants with holes, 205
Lions with toils and men with flatterers;
But when I tell him he hates flatterers,
He says he does, being then most flattered.
Let me work;
For I can give his humour the true bent, 210
And I will bring him to the Capitol.
Cassius: Nay, we will all of us be there to fetch him.
Brutus: By the eighth hour: is that the uttermost?
Cinna: Be that the uttermost, and fail not then.
Metellus: Caius Ligarius doth bear Cæsar hard, 215
Who rated him for speaking well of Pompey:
I wonder none of you have thought of him.
Brutus: Now, good Metellus, go along by him:
He loves me well, and I have given him reasons;
Send him but hither, and I'll fashion him. 220
Cassius: The morning comes upon's: we'll leave you, Brutus.
And, friends, disperse yourselves; but all remember
What you have said, and show yourselves true Romans.
Brutus: Good gentlemen, look fresh and merrily;
Let not our looks put on our purposes; 225
But bear it as our Roman actors do,
With untired spirits and formal constancy:
And so, good morrow to you every one.
                    [*Exeunt. Brutus remains.*]
Boy! Lucius! Fast asleep? It is no matter;
Enjoy the honey-heavy dew of slumber: 230
Thou hast no figures nor no fantasies,
Which busy care draws in the brains of men;
Therefore thou sleep'st so sound.

[*Enter Portia.*]

Portia: Brutus, my lord!
Brutus: Portia, what mean you? wherefore rise you now?
It is not for your health thus to commit 235
Your weak condition to the raw cold morning.
Portia: Nor for yours neither. You've ungently, Brutus,
Stole from my bed: and yesternight, at supper,
You suddenly arose and walk'd about
Musing and sighing, with your arms across; 240

246   *wafture:* wave

249   *withal:* also, at the same time
250   *an effect of humour:* a temporary mood

259   *embrace the means:* take the necessary steps

262   *humours:* dampness, mist

265   *vile ... night:* It was believed that it was easier to catch
        diseases at night because the purifying sun wasn't shining.
266   *rheumy:* cold and damp

275   *heavy:* disturbed

And when I ask'd you what the matter was,
You stared upon me with ungentle looks;
I urged you further, then you scratch'd your head,
And too impatiently stamp'd with your foot;
Yet I insisted, yet you answer'd not,   245
But, with an angry wafture of your hand,
Gave sign for me to leave you: so I did,
Fearing to strengthen that impatience
Which seem'd too much enkindled, and withal
Hoping it was but an effect of humour,   250
Which sometime hath his hour with every man.
It will not let you eat, nor talk, nor sleep
And could it work so much upon your shape
As it hath much prevail'd on your condition,
I should not know you, Brutus. Dear my lord,   255
Make me acquainted with your cause of grief.
Brutus: I am not well in health, and that is all.
Portia: Brutus is wise, and, were he not in health,
He would embrace the means to come by it.
Brutus: Why, so I do. Good Portia, go to bed.   260
Portia: Is Brutus sick? and is it physical
To walk unbraced and suck up the humours
Of the dark morning? What, is Brutus sick,
And will he steal out of his wholesome bed,
To dare the vile contagion of the night   265
And tempt the rheumy and unpurged air
To add unto his sickness? No, my Brutus;
You have some sick offence within your mind,
Which, by the right and virtue of my place,
I ought to know of, and, upon my knees,   270
I charm you, by my once commended beauty,
By all your vows of love and that great vow
Which did incorporate and make us one,
That you unfold to me, your self, your half,
Why you are heavy, and what men to-night   275
Have had resort to you: for here have been
Some six or seven, who did hide their faces
Even from darkness.
Brutus: Kneel not, gentle Portia.

289   *ruddy drops:* blood

295   *Cato:* Portia's father, Marcus Cato (95 B.C.E.–46 B.C.E.), was
        highly respected for his courage and integrity. He was
        devoted to the Republic of Rome and had fought with
        Pompey against Caesar.

299   *constancy:* capacity to endure pain and suffering

308   *charactery:* the lines and wrinkles that are written (on my
        forehead)

313   *Vouchsafe:* may I say

Portia: I should not need, if you were gentle Brutus.
   Within the bond of marriage, tell me, Brutus,   280
   Is it excepted I should know no secrets
   That appertain to you? Am I yourself
   But, as it were, in sort or limitation,
   To keep with you at meals, comfort your bed,
   And talk to you sometimes? Dwell I but in the suburbs   285
   Of your good pleasure? If it be no more,
   Portia is Brutus's harlot, not his wife.
Brutus: You are my true and honourable wife,
   As dear to me as are the ruddy drops
   That visit my sad heart.   290
Portia: If this were true, then should I know this secret.
   I grant I am a woman; but withal
   A woman that Lord Brutus took to wife:
   I grant I am a woman; but withal
   A woman well-reputed, Cato's daughter.   295
   Think you I am no stronger than my sex,
   Being so father'd and so husbanded?
   Tell me your counsels, I will not disclose 'em:
   I have made strong proof of my constancy,
   Giving myself a voluntary wound   300
   Here in the thigh: can I bear that with patience,
   And not my husband's secrets?
Brutus: O ye gods,
   Render me worthy of this noble wife!

                          [Knocking within.]
   Hark, hark! one knocks: Portia, go in awhile;
   And by and by thy bosom shall partake   305
   The secrets of my heart.
   All my engagements I will construe to thee
   All the charactery of my sad brows:
   Leave me with haste. *[Exit Portia,]* Lucius, who's that
     knocks?

[Re-enter Lucius followed by Ligarius.]

Lucius: Here is a sick man that would speak with you.   310
Brutus: Caius Ligarius, that Metellus spake of.
   Boy, stand aside, Caius Ligarius! how?
Ligarius: Vouchsafe good morrow from a feeble tongue.

315   *To wear a kerchief:* to be ill. When people were sick, they
         wore scarves or head covers for protection from drafts.

323   *exorcist:* a person who casts out evil spirits

Brutus: O, what a time have you chose out, brave Caius,
   To wear a kerchief! Would you were not sick!   315
Ligarius: I am not sick, if Brutus have in hand
   Any exploit worthy the name of honour.
Brutus: Such an exploit have I in hand, Ligarius,
   Had you a healthful ear to hear of it.
Ligarius: By all the gods that Romans bow before,   320
   I here discard my sickness! Soul of Rome?
   Brave son, derived from honourable loins!
   Thou, like an exorcist hast conjured up
   My mortified spirit. Now bid me run,
   And I will strive with things impossible;   325
   Yea, get the better of them. What's to do?
Brutus: A piece of work that will make sick men whole.
Ligarius: But are not some whole that we must make sick?
Brutus: That must we also. What it is, my Caius,
   I shall unfold to thee, as we are going   330
   To whom it must be done.
Ligarius: Set on your foot,
   And with a heart new-fired I follow you,
   To do I know not what: but it sufficeth
   That Brutus leads me on.   [*Thunder.*]
Brutus: Follow me then.   [*Exeunt.*]

Act 2, Scene 1: Activities

1. Do you think Brutus is the kind of person who would seek other people's opinions or advice? Give evidence to support your opinion.

   - What do you think about Brutus's ultimate decision and the line of reasoning he uses to reach it?
   - If you were to offer Brutus advice, what would you say to him and how would you word it? Would you present it orally or would you write it in a letter?

   Prepare your advice either as a letter or as a carefully constructed speech that you can share with the whole class.

2. After Brutus welcomes the conspirators, he and Cassius have their own private conversation. No one hears what they say to each other. Imagine you are in a position to eavesdrop on the discussion. Create a dialogue between Cassius and Brutus. Write your dialogue as a script and perform it for other groups or for the whole class.

3. Cassius has specifically selected the Ides of March as the time for Caesar's assassination. Do some research to find out why this date is so significant to the Romans and why it plays such a key role in the play. Write a detailed essay in which you link your findings to actual events in the play.

4. As well as making his decision to murder Caesar, Brutus makes a number of other decisions in the scene. With a partner, brainstorm a list of these decisions, check your list against the text for accuracy, and then determine how these decisions affect your perceptions of Brutus as a man. Include this information in a detailed character sketch in which you bring out the complexities of this person. You can include these insights about him in a profile that you could continue to develop for the rest of the play.

5. Though they don't seem to have thought much about it themselves so far, do you think Brutus and the other conspirators would make sound leaders of a government in Rome? Discuss this in your groups and then write a political commentary for a Roman newspaper explaining why you think they would or would not create a superior government to one run by Caesar alone.

6. Most people have some superstitions about weather that they either believe or know about because they are commonly held to have an effect on our lives. In your group, brainstorm some of these superstitions or observations. How many of them have any scientific basis and how many of them do you actually believe?

Shakespeare treats the Romans as superstitious people when it comes to weather, though it may well be that he is simply reflecting the Elizabethans themselves. Research some "weather beliefs" from these two periods and in an essay, determine how Shakespeare uses them as almost another character in the play.

For the next scene ...

Have you ever been flattered by another person or group of people? What were the circumstances and how did you react? Record your experience in your journal. Explain how you think flattery can be a positive influence on a person and how it might be a negative one.

Act 2, Scene 2

In this scene ...

We discover a sleepless Caesar troubled by the raging storm and Calpurnia's dreams of his murder. After asking the augurers (priests who interpret omens) to predict his fortune for that day, he says that he plans to go to the Capitol despite his wife's pleadings for him to stay home. Even after he hears the report from the augurers warning him not "to stir forth today," Caesar states that he is still not afraid. Nevertheless, he soon bows to Calpurnia's wishes. Decius arrives, however, and convinces Caesar that he *must* go to the Capitol. When the rest of the conspirators enter, Caesar greets them graciously, and soon they leave for the Capitol.

6   *success:* the result of the sacrifice. Priests would sacrifice animals to the gods and interpret the appearance of the entrails (inner organs) to predict the future.

10–12   *Caesar ... vanished:* This is often viewed as an expression of Caesar's hubris (pride) in that it represents an overconfidence in his own personal powers and abilities.

13   *stood on ceremonies:* believed in omens

25   *beyond all use:* unnatural, beyond everything we are accustomed to seeing

Scene 2

The same. A room in Cæsar's house.
Thunder and lightning. Enter Cæsar
in his nightgown.

Cæsar: Nor heaven nor earth have been at peace tonight:
　Thrice hath Calpurnia in her sleep cried out,
　"Help, ho! they murder Cæsar!" Who's within?

[*Enter a Servant.*]

Servant: My lord?
Cæsar: Go bid the priests do present sacrifice　　　　　　5
　And bring me their opinions of success.
Servant: I will, my lord.　　　　　　　　　　　[*Exit.*]

[*Enter Calpurnia.*]

Calpurnia: What mean you, Cæsar? think you to walk forth?
　You shall not stir out of your house to-day.
Cæsar: Cæsar shall forth: the things that threaten'd me　　10
　Ne'er look'd but on my back; when they shall see
　The face of Cæsar, they are vanished.
Calpurnia: Cæsar, I never stood on ceremonies,
　Yet now they fright me. There is one within,
　Besides the things that we have heard and seen,　　　　15
　Recounts most horrid sights seen by the watch.
　A lioness hath whelped in the streets;
　And graves have yawn'd, and yielded up their dead;
　Fierce fiery warriors fought upon the clouds,
　In ranks and squadrons and right form of war　　　　20
　Which drizzled blood upon the Capitol;
　The noise of battle hurtled in the air,
　Horses did neigh, and dying men did groan,
　And ghosts did shriek and squeal about the streets,
　O Cæsar! these things are beyond all use,　　　　　　25

28   *Caesar:* Heads of state commonly referred to themselves in the third person; it was an accepted convention.

30–31   *When beggars ... princes:* This refers to the Elizabethan view that nature reflects and parallels events happening in the lives of people. In literature, this is called "pathetic fallacy."

42   *without a heart:* The heart was thought to be the organ of courage; here the meaning is "cowardly."

And I do fear them.
Cæsar: What can be avoided
  Whose end is purposed by the mighty gods?
  Yet Cæsar shall go forth; for these predictions
  Are to the world in general as to Cæsar.
Calpurnia: When beggars die, there are no comets seen;   30
  The heavens themselves blaze forth the death of princes.
Cæsar: Cowards die many times before their deaths;
  The valiant never taste of death but once.
  Of all the wonders that I yet have heard,
  It seems to me most strange that men should fear;   35
  Seeing that death, a necessary end,
  Will come when it will come.

[*Re-enter Servant.*]

                      What say the augurers?
Servant: They would not have you to stir forth to-day.
  Plucking the entrails of an offering forth,
  They could not find a heart within the beast.   40
Cæsar: The gods do this in shame of cowardice:
  Cæsar should be a beast without a heart,
  If he should stay at home to-day for fear.
  No, Cæsar shall not: danger knows full well
  That Cæsar is more dangerous than he: 45
  We are two lions litter'd in one day,
  And I the elder and more terrible:
  And Cæsar shall go forth.
Calpurnia: Alas, my lord,
  Your wisdom is consumed in confidence.
  Do not go forth to-day: call it my fear   50
  That keeps you in the house, and not your own.
  We'll send Mark Antony to the senate-house;
  And he shall say you are not well to-day:
  Let me, upon my knee, prevail in this.
Cæsar: Mark Antony shall say I am not well;   55
  And for thy humour, I will stay at home.

[*Enter Decius.*]

Here's Decius Brutus, he shall tell them so.
Decius: Cæsar, all hail! good morrow, worthy Cæsar:

60   *happy time:* just the right moment

87–88 *great Rome ... blood:* This refers to the practice of people dipping cloths into the blood of slain martyrs (those who die in great suffering for their beliefs) for keepsakes and remembrances.

89   *tinctures:* dyes or colours as in a medicinal solution; *stains:* a discolouration or dye; *relics:* objects of reverence; *cognizance:* distinguishing badge of service

96–97 *a mock ... render'd:* likely to be misinterpreted and laughed at

I come to fetch you to the senate-house.

Cæsar: And you are come in very happy time,   60
    To bear my greeting to the senators
    And tell them that I will not come to-day:
    Cannot, is false, and that I dare not, falser:
    I will not come to-day: tell them so, Decius.

Calpurnia: Say he is sick.

Cæsar: Shall Cæsar send a lie?   65
    Have I in conquest stretch'd mine arm so far,
    To be afeard to tell greybeards the truth?
    Decius, go tell them Cæsar will not come.

Decius: Most mighty Cæsar, let me know some cause,
    Lest I be laugh'd at when I tell them so.   70

Cæsar: The cause is in my will: I will not come;
    That is enough to satisfy the senate.
    But for your private satisfaction,
    Because I love you, I will let you know.
    Calpurnia here, my wife, stays me at home: 75
    She dreamt to-night she saw my statue,
    Which, like a fountain with an hundred spouts,
    Did run pure blood; and many lusty Romans
    Came smiling, and did bathe their hands in it:
    And these does she apply for warnings, and portents,   80
    And evils imminent: and on her knee
    Hath begg'd that I will stay at home to-day.

Decius: This dream is all amiss interpreted;
    It was a vision fair and fortunate:
    Your statue spouting blood in many pipes,   85
    In which so many smiling Romans bathed,
    Signifies that from you great Rome shall suck
    Reviving blood, and that great men shall press
    For tinctures, stains, relics, and cognizance.
    This by Calpurnia's dream is signified.   90

Cæsar: And this way have you well expounded it.

Decius: I have, when you have heard what I can say:
    And know it now: the senate have concluded
    To give this day a crown to mighty Cæsar.
    If you shall send them word you will not come,   95
    Their minds may change. Besides, it were a mock
    Apt to be render'd, for some one to say

103   *proceeding:* advancement of your career

112   *enemy:* Caesar had pardoned Caius Ligarius for having supported Pompey.

113   *ague:* disease or sickness

129   *yearns:* grieves

"Break up the senate till another time,
When Cæsar's wife shall meet with better dreams."
If Cæsar hide himself, shall they not whisper,   100
"Lo, Cæsar is afraid"?
Pardon me, Cæsar; for my dear, dear love
To your proceeding bids me tell you this,
And reason to my love is liable.
Cæsar: How foolish do your fears seem now, Calpurnia!   105
   I am ashamed I did yield to them.
   Give me my robe, for I will go.

   [*Enter Publius, Brutus, Ligarius, Metellus, Casca, Trebonius,
    and Cinna.*]

   And look where Publius is come to fetch me.
Publius: Good morrow, Cæsar.
Cæsar: Welcome, Publius.
   What, Brutus, are you stirr'd so early too?   110
   Good morrow, Casca, Caius Ligarius,
   Cæsar was ne'er so much your enemy
   As that same ague which hath made you lean.
   What is't o'clock?
Brutus: Cæsar, 'tis strucken eight.
Cæsar: I thank you for your pains and courtesy.   115

   [*Enter Antony.*]

   See! Antony, that revels long o'nights,
   Is notwithstanding up. Good morrow, Antony.
Antony: So to most noble Cæsar.
Cæsar: Bid them prepare within:
   I am to blame to be thus waited for.
   Now, Cinna: now, Metellus: what, Trebonius!   120
   I have an hour's talk in store for you;
   Remember that you call on me to-day:
   Be near me, that I may remember you.
Trebonius: Cæsar, I will: [*Aside*] and so near will I be,
   That your best friends shall wish I had been further.   125
Cæsar: Good friends, go in, and taste some wine with me;
   And we, like friends, will straightway go together.
Brutus [*Aside*]: That every like is not the same, O Cæsar,
   The heart of Brutus yearns to think upon!   [*Exeunt.*]

Act 2, Scene 2: Activities

1. So far in the play we have seen several aspects of Caesar:

   - a great military hero
   - a political leader and ruler of people
   - a friend and husband
   - a man, subject to the same fears and doubts most people share

   In groups, consider the above aspects of Caesar's life; find and record evidence from this scene that supports these parts of his character. You may want to do this in chart form or as a map to keep things in perspective.

2. If you could "walk into" this scene and have a chance to warn Caesar about the conspirators' plans, what would you say to him?

   - How would you explain the real meaning behind the seemingly friendly words and actions of the conspirators?
   - How would you present your information to Caesar so he would listen to you and ultimately believe you?

   Role-play your speech for your class having another class member play an unsuspecting Caesar. Be sure to explain or make known to your audience the point where this speech would be inserted.

3. Flattery and deception seem to work in certain situations with certain people. In your journal, record an incident in which you have seen this happen.

   Find several examples of flattery in this play and determine what effect giving in to the flattery ultimately has on the people involved. How does this affect any of the actions that follow?

4. In the past, there have been assassinations of famous leaders. Choose one of these people and research the events that happened just before this person's death. You might consider the following as guides while you do your research:

- Who were the people who saw the leader as a threat to their well-being?
- Did the leader have any warnings about impending danger? If so, where did these warnings come from? If you do not know, speculate how the person might have felt about and responded to these warning signals.
- What was the effect of the assassination on the country and on people in the rest of the world?

Prepare a written, oral, and visual account of your findings for presentation to the whole class as an Independent Study Unit.

5. Dramatic irony happens when the play's audience knows something that some or all of the characters don't know anything about. Its purpose is to heighten tension and create a sense of anticipation.

Find as many instances as you can where dramatic irony occurs in this scene. As a director, explain to your actors why you think it is essential that they understand it so they can present a performance of the play that has maximum impact on the audience. Prepare this as a speech you might give to your cast, and deliver it to your group for their response.

For the next scenes ...

If you were Caesar, would you have rejected the warnings against going to the Capitol? Explain your response.

Act 2, Scenes 3 and 4

In these scenes ...

While Caesar and his escorts are setting out from his house, we meet Artemidorus standing on a street that Caesar will follow to the Capitol. Artemidorus is reading a letter that could save Caesar's life. He plans to hand Caesar the letter as Caesar passes by.

In another part of the street we see Portia, who now seems aware of what the conspirators, led by her husband, plan to do. She orders the servant Lucius to run to the senate house and bring back news of what is happening. The Soothsayer passes Portia on his way to the Capitol and states his intention to tell Caesar again about his fears of what may happen on the Ides of March.

7   *security:* overconfidence

9   *lover:* dear friend

11   *suitor:* one who brings forward a case or request to a legal
     council or government
13   *emulation:* attempt to equal or excel

15   *contrive:* conspire

Scene 3

The same. A street near the Capitol.
Enter Artemidorus, reading a paper.

Artemidorus: Cæsar, beware of Brutus; take heed of Cassius;
    come not near Casca; have an eye to Cinna; trust not
    Trebonius; mark well Metellus Cimber: Decius Brutus
    loves thee not: thou hast wronged Caius Ligarius.
    There is but one mind in all these men, and it is bent   5
    against Cæsar. If thou beest not immortal, look about
    you; security gives way to conspiracy. The mighty gods
    defend thee!

                              Thy lover, *Artemidorus.*

Here will I stand till Cæsar pass along,   10
And as a suitor will I give him this.
My heart laments that virtue cannot live
Out of the teeth of emulation.
If thou read this, O Cæsar, thou mayst live;
If not, the Fates with traitors do contrive.   [*Exit.*]   15

6   *constancy:* self-control, strength

9   *keep counsel:* keep secrets

18   *rumour:* confused noise; *fray:* battle

20   *Sooth:* truly

Scene 4

Another part of the same street,
before the house of Brutus.
Enter Portia and Lucius.

Portia: I prithee, boy, run to the senate-house,
   Stay not to answer me, but get thee gone:
   Why dost thou stay?
Lucius: To know my errand, madam.
Portia: I would have had thee there, and here again,
   Ere I can tell thee what thou shouldst do there.   5
   O constancy, be strong upon my side!
   Set a huge mountain 'tween my heart and tongue!
   I have a man's mind, but a woman's might.
   How hard it is for women to keep counsel!
   Art thou here yet?
Lucius: Madam, what should I do?   10
   Run to the Capitol, and nothing else?
   And so return to you, and nothing else?
Portia: Yes, bring me word, boy, if thy lord look well,
   For he went sickly forth: and take good note
   What Cæsar doth, what suitors press to him.   15
   Hark, boy! what noise is that?
Lucius: I hear none, madam.
Portia: Prithee, listen well;
   I heard a bustling rumour, like a fray,
   And the wind brings it from the Capitol.
Lucius: Sooth, madam, I hear nothing.   20

   [*Enter the Soothsayer.*]

Portia: Come hither, fellow: which way hast thou been?
Soothsayer: At mine own house, good lady.
Portia: What is't o'clock?
Soothsayer: About the ninth hour, lady.
Portia: Is Cæsar yet gone to the Capitol?

27   *suit:* important message or matter of concern

37   *void:* empty

42–43   *Brutus ... grant:* Portia makes up an excuse for her anxiety
        in case Lucius has overheard her.
44   *commend:* give my love
45   *merry:* cheerful

Soothsayer: Madam, not yet: I go to take my stand,   25
  To see him pass on to the Capitol.
Portia: Thou hast some suit to Cæsar, hast thou not?
Soothsayer: That I have, lady: if it will please Cæsar
  To be so good to Cæsar as to hear me,
  I shall beseech him to befriend himself.   30
Portia: Why, know'st thou any harm's intended towards
  him?
Soothsayer: None that I know will be, much that I fear
  may chance.
  Good morrow to you. Here the street is narrow:
  The throng that follows Cæsar at the heels,
  Of senators, of prætors, common suitors,   35
  Will crowd a feeble man almost to death:
  I'll get me to a place more void, and there
  Speak to great Cæsar as he comes along.   *[Exit.]*
Portia: I must go in. Ay me, how weak a thing
  The heart of woman is! O Brutus,   40
  The heavens speed thee in thine enterprise!
  Sure, the boy heard me. Brutus hath a suit
  That Cæsar will not grant. O, I grow faint.
  Run, Lucius, and commend me to my lord;
  Say I am merry: come to me again,   45
  And bring me word what he doth say to thee.
                    [Exeunt severally.]

Act 2, Scenes 3 and 4: Activities

1. Much seems to have gone on since we last encountered Portia, who appears to be very agitated in Scene 4. In your journal, determine what you think might have happened in the interim, or discuss this with a partner or a group.

   Once you have reached your decision, imagine you have received a phone call from Portia who needs help to cope with her situation. What advice do you give her and how do you help to calm her? Do any soap operas come to mind? Write your response to her as either a private journal entry or as a follow-up letter or e-mail to her call.

2. Some people argue that these two scenes are irrelevant to the play. They feel that having Artemidorus appear out of nowhere is preposterous and that having Portia suddenly reduced to a state of paranoia is absurd. Would you eliminate these two scenes? If you did, what if anything would you use to connect Act 2, Scene 2 with Act 3? Write a 500-word critical essay using persuasive arguments in support of your point of view.

3. Suppose there was a "lost" scene between Brutus and Portia in which he revealed that he was involved in a plot to kill Caesar. Where would this scene likely occur, under what circumstances, and what might their conversation sound like? Write this dialogue and enact it for the class.

4. After examining Portia's behaviour in Scene 4, in your group discuss qualities of her personality that you find particularly admirable and/or disturbing. Create a profile of Portia in your journal based on these impressions. Have your impressions of Portia changed from the ones you had in Act 2, Scene 1? Add your response to this question in your journal entry.

Act 2: Consider the Whole Act

1. Imagine that a friend returns to school after missing the study of Act 2. You want to give him or her information about what has happened since the end of Act 1. What dialogue and action highlights would you include in your update?

2. With the assistance of your teacher or librarian, locate books with illustrations of ancient Roman settings. Select one or more pictures that might be appropriate for a section of a scene in this act. Using details from the picture(s), draw or write about the setting. Present your result to your group. You might make a collection of your settings for a class viewing.

3. In Act 2, we observe the wives of both Brutus and Caesar expressing concern for their husbands' safety and well-being. Today, the spouses of many political leaders play important roles in the leaders' public lives.

   Choose one partnership you know in which the spouse plays an active role in the political figure's public life.

   Prepare a set of questions you would ask the spouse if you could interview him or her for a radio or television program. Phrase the questions so they will require the person being interviewed to reveal as much of his or her personality as possible.

4. *Make a video*

   This activity is done in pairs or small groups. Select a part of a scene in this act in which you focus on the difficulty the two characters have accepting what each other is saying. Working in pairs or small groups, use the camera to create a mood.

   Rehearse the speeches a few times to be sure you are clear about the meaning of the lines, the words, the movement, and the interaction.

Prepare a shooting script or storyboard in which you do the following:

- Consider the distance between the camera and the subject that would be appropriate for each shot.
- Determine the kind of lighting you think will best convey the mood you are seeking to create.
- Provide one shot per complete thought.

Have other members of the class judge how successful you have been in conveying mood through your video presentation.

5. If we treat ethics and values equally, then we never have to be concerned about which one we have to sacrifice to save the other. Define what you understand these terms to mean. The play seems to blur ethics and values in disturbing ways. In a 500-word essay, decide what punishment is reserved for those leaders who would force us to make such a choice in the first place. Where do Cassius, Brutus, and Caesar stand on this issue, and where, ultimately, do the people stand when facing this issue?

For the next scene ...

Have you ever ignored the advice of others to do something your way? What happened? What would have happened if you had followed the advice given?

What are some possible ways the disastrous events of the Ides of March might have been prevented?

Act 3, Scene 1

In this scene ...

Ignoring all warnings, Caesar goes to the Capitol and begins to deal with the business of state as usual. The conspirators attack him as planned, and Caesar falls dead at the base of Pompey's statue.

After the murder, the conspirators proclaim "Liberty! Freedom!" but the other senators and the citizens, especially, are confused and afraid. Brutus quickly tries to calm them but isn't too successful, considering that the conspirators are washing their hands in Caesar's blood.

Antony's servant arrives wanting assurance that Antony himself will not be killed. Brutus assures him that Antony will not be harmed.

Antony appears, makes a great display of mourning over Caesar's body, and listens to Brutus and Cassius promise to protect him from harm and to guarantee him the right to speak freely at Caesar's funeral.

When left alone, Antony lets everyone know that he is not loyal to the conspirators. In the midst of this, a messenger announces that Octavius Caesar, the slain Caesar's grand-nephew and designated heir, is about to arrive with his army in Rome. Antony warns that Rome is too dangerous a place for Octavius and that he should wait until after the funeral.

Antony leaves the Capitol with his servant, the two of them carrying Caesar's body to the public marketplace.

3   *schedule:* scroll or paper

18   *makes:* makes his way
19   *be sudden:* be on your guard

Act 3, Scene 1

Rome. Before the Capitol; the
Senate sitting above.

A crowd of people; among them
Artemidorus and the Soothsayer.
Flourish. Enter Cæsar, Brutus,
Cassius, Casca, Decius, Metellus,
Trebonius, Cinna, Antony,
Lepidus, Popilius, Publius,
and others.

Cæsar [*To the Soothsayer*]: The Ides of March are come.
Soothsayer: Ay, Cæsar; but not gone.
Artemidorus: Hail, Cæsar! read this schedule.
Decius: Trebonius doth desire you to o'er-read,
    At your best leisure, this his humble suit.   5
Artemidorus: O Cæsar, read mine first; for mine's a suit
    That touches Cæsar nearer: read it, great Cæsar.
Cæsar: What touches us ourself shall be last served.
Artemidorus: Delay not, Cæsar; read it instantly.
Cæsar: What, is the fellow mad?
Publius: Sirrah, give place.   10
Cassius: What, urge you your petitions in the street?
    Come to the Capitol.
        [*Cæsar goes up to the Senate-House, the rest following.*]
Popilius: I wish your enterprise to-day may thrive.
Cassius: What enterprise, Popilius?
Popilius: Fare you well.
                     [*Advances to Cæsar.*]
Brutus: What said Popilius Lena?   15
Cassius: He wish'd to-day our enterprise might thrive.
    I fear our purpose is discovered.
Brutus: Look, how he makes to Cæsar: mark him.
Cassius: Casca, be sudden, for we fear prevention.

| 21 | *turn back:* return alive |

| 25 | *knows his time:* is acting according to the plan |

| 28 | *presently prefer:* immediately present |
| 29 | *address'd:* present |

| 33 | *puissant:* powerful |

| 36 | *couchings ... courtesies:* bowings and bending low |

| 38–39 | *turn ... children:* make long established laws and customs like rules for children's games |
| 39–42 | *Be not ... fools:* Do not be foolish enough to think that Caesar's spirit can be convinced to rebel against his true nature by that which persuades fools. |

| 51 | *repealing:* recalling |

| 54 | *freedom of repeal:* liberation from exile |

Brutus, what shall be done? If this be known,   20
  Cassius or Cæsar never shall turn back,
  For I will slay myself.
Brutus: Cassius, be constant:
  Popilius Lena speaks not of our purposes;
  For, look, he smiles, and Cæsar doth not change.
Cassius: Trebonius knows his time; for, look you, Brutus,   25
  He draws Mark Antony out of the way.
                        [*Exeunt Antony and Trebonius.*]
Decius: Where is Metellus Cimber? Let him go,
  And presently prefer his suit to Cæsar.
Brutus: He is address'd: press near and second him.
Cinna: Casca, you are the first that rears your hand.   30
Cæsar: Are we all ready? What is now amiss
  That Cæsar and his senate must redress?
Metellus: Most high, most mighty, and most puissant Cæsar,
  Metellus Cimber throws before thy seat
  An humble heart:—   [*Kneeling.*]
Cæsar: I must prevent thee, Cimber.   35
  These couchings and these lowly courtesies
  Might fire the blood of ordinary men,
  And turn pre-ordinance and first decree
  Into the law of children. Be not fond,
  To think that Cæsar bears such rebel blood   40
  That will be thaw'd from the true quality
  With that which melteth fools; I mean, sweet words,
  Low-crooked court'sies and base spaniel-fawning.
  Thy brother by decree is banished:
  If thou dost bend and pray and fawn for him,   45
  I spurn thee like a cur out of my way.
  Know, Cæsar doth not wrong nor without cause
  Will he be satisfied.
Metellus: Is there no voice more worthy than my own,
  To sound more sweetly in great Cæsar's ear,   50
  For the repealing of my banish'd brother?
Brutus: I kiss thy hand, but not in flattery, Cæsar;
  Desiring thee that Publius Cimber may
  Have an immediate freedom of repeal.
Cæsar: What, Brutus!
Cassius: Pardon, Cæsar; Cæsar, pardon;   55

57   *enfranchisement:* freedom

60   *northern star:* the Pole star that seemed to remain stable in
          the sky and which was used universally by sailors as the
          reference point for navigation because it never changed
          position

67   *apprehensive:* capable of reasoning, understanding

69   *holds on his rank:* keeps his position

74   *Olympus:* In Greek mythology this was a mountain in
          Greece where the gods lived.
75   *bootless:* in vain

77   *Et tu, Brute!:* And you, too, Brutus!

80   *common pulpits:* platform for public speakers in the Forum

83   *ambition's debt:* the price to be paid for ambition

86   *confounded:* overwhelmed

89   *standing:* organizing a resistance or opposition

As low as to thy foot doth Cassius fall,
To beg enfranchisement for Publius Cimber.
Cæsar: I would be well moved, if I were as you;
If I could pray to move, prayers would move me:
But I am constant as the northern star,   60
Of whose true-fix'd and resting quality
There is no fellow in the firmament.
The skies are painted with unnumber'd sparks;
They are all fire and every one doth shine;
But there's but one in all doth hold his place: 65
So in the world; 'tis furnish'd well with men,
And men are flesh and blood, and apprehensive;
Yet in the number I do know but one
That unassailable holds on his rank,
Unshaked of motion: and that I am he,   70
Let me a little show it, even in this;
That I was constant Cimber should be banish'd,
And constant do remain to keep him so.
Cinna: O Cæsar,——
Cæsar: Hence! wilt thou lift up Olympus?
Decius: Great Cæsar,——
Cæsar: Doth not Brutus bootless kneel?   75
Casca: Speak, hands, for me!
    [*Casca first, then the other Conspirators, and last Marcus Brutus
        stab Cæsar.*]
Cæsar: Et tu, Brute! Then fall, Cæsar!   [*Dies.*]
Cinna: Liberty! Freedom! Tyranny is dead!
    Run hence, proclaim, cry it about the streets.
Cassius: Some to the common pulpits, and cry out   80
    "Liberty, freedom, and enfranchisement!"
Brutus: People, and senators, be not affrighted;
    Fly not; stand still: ambition's debt is paid.
Casca: Go to the pulpit, Brutus.
Decius: And Cassius too.
Brutus: Where's Publius?   85
Cinna: Here, quite confounded with this mutiny.
Metellus: Stand fast together, lest some friend of Cæsar's
    Should chance——
Brutus: Talk not of standing. Publius, good cheer;
    There is no harm intended to your person,   90

94   *abide:* suffer the consequences of

104   *abridged:* shortened

115   *Pompey's basis:* the base of the statue of Pompey, where Caesar fell

120   *grace his heels:* honour him by following on his heels

Nor to no Roman else: so tell them, Publius.
Cassius: And leave us, Publius; lest that the people,
    Rushing on us, should do your age some mischief.
Brutus: Do so: and let no man abide this deed,
    But we the doers.

    [*Re-enter Trebonius.*]

Cassius: Where is Antony?   95
Trebonius: Fled to his house amazed:
    Men, wives and children stare, cry out and run
    As it were doomsday.
Brutus: Fates, we will know your pleasures:
    That we shall die, we know; 'tis but the time
    And drawing days out, that men stand upon.   100
Cassius: Why, he that cuts off twenty years of life
    Cuts off so many years of fearing death.
Brutus: Grant that, and then is death a benefit:
    So are we Cæsar's friends, that have abridged
    His time of fearing death. Stoop, Romans, stoop,   105
    And let us bathe our hands in Cæsar's blood
    Up to the elbows, and besmear our swords:
    Then walk we forth, even to the market-place,
    And, waving our red weapons o'er our heads,
    Let's all cry "Peace, freedom, and liberty!"   110
Cassius: Stoop then, and wash. How many ages hence
    Shall this our lofty scene be acted over
    In states unborn and accents yet unknown!
Brutus: How many times shall Cæsar bleed in sport,
    That now on Pompey's basis lies along   115
    No worthier than the dust!
Cassius: So oft as that shall be,
    So often shall the knot of us be call'd
    The men that gave their country liberty.
Decius: What, shall we forth?
Cassius: Ay, every man away:
    Brutus shall lead; and we will grace his heels   120
    With the most boldest and best hearts of Rome.

    [*Enter a Servant.*]

Brutus: Soft! who comes here? A friend of Antony's.

131   *be resolved:* be informed to his satisfaction

136   *this untrod state:* new and confusing state of affairs

146   *Falls ... purpose:* proves to be uncomfortably correct ("to
       the purpose")

152   *let blood:* killed. Surgeons would let or draw blood from a
       patient to purge or cleanse the person of disease. *rank:*
       Here, rank combines three meanings: corrupted by disease
       (a continuation of the medical reference in "let blood");
       overgrown (too powerful); and of the same position or
       degree as Caesar.

Servant: Thus, Brutus, did my master bid me kneel;
  Thus did Mark Antony bid me fall down;
  And, being prostrate, thus he bade me say: 125
  Brutus is noble, wise, valiant and honest;
  Cæsar was mighty, bold, royal, and loving:
  Say I love Brutus and I honour him;
  Say I fear'd Cæsar, honour'd him and loved him.
  If Brutus will vouchsafe that Antony   130
  May safely come to him, and be resolved
  How Cæsar hath deserved to lie in death,
  Mark Antony shall not love Cæsar dead
  So well as Brutus living; but will follow
  The fortunes and affairs of noble Brutus   135
  Thorough the hazards of this untrod state
  With all true faith. So says my master Antony.
Brutus: Thy master is a wise and valiant Roman;
  I never thought him worse.
  Tell him, so please him come unto this place,   140
  He shall be satisfied, and, by my honour,
  Depart untouch'd.
Servant: I'll fetch him presently.   [*Exit.*]
Brutus: I know that we shall have him well to friend.
Cassius: I wish we may: but yet have I a mind
  That fears him much; and my misgiving still   145
  Falls shrewdly to the purpose.
Brutus: But here comes Antony.

  [*Re-enter Antony.*]

                      Welcome, Mark Antony.
Antony: O mighty Cæsar! dost thou lie so low?
  Are all thy conquests, glories, triumphs, spoils,
  Shrunk to this little measure? Fare thee well.   150
  I know not, gentlemen, what you intend,
  Who else must be let blood, who else is rank:
  If I myself, there is no hour so fit
  As Cæsar's death's hour, nor no instrument
  Of half that worth as those your swords, made rich   155
  With the most noble blood of all this world.
  I do beseech ye, if you bear me hard,
  Now, whilst your purpled hands do reek and smoke,

159	*Fulfil your pleasure:* Do with me what you wish.
160	*apt:* ready
161	*mean:* means

171	*As fire ... pity:* As one fire puts out another, so did our pity for Rome drive out our pity for Caesar.
173	*have leaden points:* are harmless
174	*in strength of malice:* with the same strength as if we were enemies
175	*temper:* attitude; that is, with the affection of brothers
178	*dignities:* honours, offices

191	*credit:* reputation
192	*conceit:* judge

Fulfil your pleasure. Live a thousand years,
I shall not find myself so apt to die: 160
No place will please me so, no mean of death,
As here by Cæsar, and by you cut off,
The choice and master spirits of this age.
Brutus: O Antony, beg not your death of us.
Though now we must appear bloody and cruel,   165
As, by our hands and this our present act,
You see we do, yet see you but our hands
And this the bleeding business they have done:
Our hearts you see not; they are pitiful;
And pity to the general wrong of Rome—   170
As fire drives out fire, so pity pity—
Hath done this deed on Cæsar. For your part,
To you our swords have leaden points, Mark Antony:
Our arms in strength of malice, and our hearts
Of brothers' temper, do receive you in   175
With all kind love, good thoughts and reverence.
Cassius: Your voice shall be as strong as any man's
In the disposing of new dignities.
Brutus: Only be patient till we have appeased
The multitude, beside themselves with fear,   180
And then we will deliver you the cause,
Why I, that did love Cæsar when I struck him,
Have thus proceeded.
Antony: I doubt not of your wisdom.
Let each man render me his bloody hand:
First, Marcus Brutus, will I shake with you: 185
Next, Caius Cassius, do I take your hand;
Now, Decius Brutus, yours; now yours, Metellus;
Yours, Cinna; and my valiant Casca, yours;
Though last, not least in love, yours, good Trebonius.
Gentlemen all,—alas, what shall I say?   190
My credit now stands on such slippery ground,
That one of two bad ways you must conceit me,
Either a coward or a flatterer.
That I did love thee, Cæsar, O, 'tis true:
If then thy spirit look upon us now,   195
Shall it not grieve thee dearer than thy death,
To see thy Antony making his peace,

202   *close:* enter into an agreement

204   *bay'd, brave hart:* hunted and trapped, courageous stag

206   *Sign'd in thy spoil:* marked by your blood; *lethe:* lifeblood.
        In Greek mythology, the Lethe was the river in Hades, the
        underworld. When people drank from it, they forgot
        everything about their lives on earth.

213   *modesty:* understatement

215   *compact:* agreement
216   *prick'd in number:* counted as one of

228   *Produce:* bring

Shaking the bloody fingers of thy foes,
Most noble! in the presence of thy corse?
Had I as many eyes as thou hast wounds,   200
Weeping as fast as they stream forth thy blood,
It would become me better than to close
In terms of friendship with thine enemies.
Pardon me, Julius! Here wast thou bay'd, brave hart;
Here didst thou fall, and here thy hunters stand,   205
Sign'd in thy spoil, and crimson'd in thy lethe.
O world, thou wast the forest to this hart;
And this, indeed, O world, the heart of thee.
How like a deer, strucken by many princes,
Dost thou here lie!   210
Cassius: Mark Antony——
Antony: Pardon me, Caius Cassius;
   The enemies of Cæsar shall say this;
   Then, in a friend, it is cold modesty.
Cassius: I blame you not for praising Cæsar so;
   But what compact mean you to have with us?   215
   Will you be prick'd in number of our friends,
   Or shall we on, and not depend on you?
Antony: Therefore I took your hands, but was indeed
   Sway'd from the point, by looking down on Cæsar.
   Friends am I with you all and love you all,   220
   Upon this hope, that you shall give me reasons
   Why and wherein Cæsar was dangerous.
Brutus: Or else were this a savage spectacle:
   Our reasons are so full of good regard
   That were you, Antony, the son of Cæsar,   225
   You should be satisfied.
Antony: That's all I seek:
   And am moreover suitor that I may
   Produce his body to the market-place;
   And in the pulpit, as becomes a friend,
   Speak in the order of his funeral.   230
Brutus: You shall, Mark Antony.
Cassius: Brutus, a word with you.
   [*Aside to Brutus.*] You know not what you do:
     do not consent
   That Antony speak in his funeral:

238   *protest:* announce

243   *what may fall:* what might result

257   *tide of times:* course of history

264   cumber: burden, weigh down

269   *choked ... deeds:* smothered by the familiarity of terrible acts
270   *ranging:* searching widely, hunting

Know you how much the people may be moved
By that which he will utter?
Brutus: By your pardon;   235
   I will myself into the pulpit first,
   And show the reason of our Cæsar's death:
   What Antony shall speak, I will protest
   He speaks by leave and by permission,
   And that we are contented Cæsar shall   240
   Have all true rites and lawful ceremonies.
   It shall advantage more than do us wrong.
Cassius: I know not what may fall; I like it not.
Brutus: Mark Antony, here, take you Cæsar's body.
   You shall not in your funeral speech blame us,   245
   But speak all good you can devise of Cæsar,
   And say you do't by our permission;
   Else shall you not have any hand at all
   About his funeral: and you shall speak
   In the same pulpit whereto I am going,   250
   After my speech is ended.
Antony: Be it so;
   I do desire no more.
Brutus: Prepare the body then, and follow us.
                        [Exeunt. Antony remains.]
Antony: O, pardon me, thou bleeding piece of earth,
   That I am meek and gentle with these butchers!   255
   Thou art the ruins of the noblest man
   That ever lived in the tide of times.
   Woe to the hand that shed this costly blood!
   Over thy wounds now do I prophesy,
   Which, like dumb mouths, do ope their ruby lips,   260
   To beg the voice and utterance of my tongue,
   A curse shall light upon the limbs of men;
   Domestic fury and fierce civil strife
   Shall cumber all the parts of Italy;
   Blood and destruction shall be so in use,   265
   And dreadful objects so familiar,
   That mothers shall but smile when they behold
   Their infants quarter'd with the hands of war;
   All pity choked with custom of fell deeds:
   And Cæsar's spirit, ranging for revenge,   270

271   *Até:* the goddess of revenge

273   *Cry "Havoc":* Give the signal for mass slaughter and
           looting. (Only a king could give this signal to troops.)

292   *try:* test

294   *issue:* results
295   *discourse:* relate, describe

With Até by his side come hot from hell,
Shall in these confines with a monarch's voice
Cry "Havoc!" and let slip the dogs of war;
That this foul deed shall smell above the earth
With carrion men, groaning for burial.   275

[*Enter a Servant.*]

You serve Octavius Cæsar, do you not?
Servant: I do, Mark Antony.
Antony: Cæsar did write for him to come to Rome.
Servant: He did receive his letters, and is coming;
   And bid me say to you by word of mouth——   280
   O Cæsar!——   [*Seeing the body.*]
Antony: Thy heart is big, get thee apart and weep.
   Passion, I see, is catching; for mine eyes
   Seeing those beads of sorrow stand in thine,
   Began to water. Is thy master coming?   285
Servant: He lies to-night within seven leagues of Rome.
Antony: Post back with speed, and tell him what hath
      chanced:
   Here is a mourning Rome, a dangerous Rome,
   No Rome of safety for Octavius yet;
   Hie hence, and tell him so. Yet, stay awhile;   290
   Thou shalt not back till I have borne this corse
   Into the market-place: there shall I try,
   In my oration, how the people take
   The cruel issue of these bloody men;
   According to the which, thou shalt discourse   295
   To young Octavius of the state of things.
   Lend me your hand.   [*Exeunt with Cæsar's body.*]

Act 3, Scene 1: Activities

1. Imagine that you are a senator of Rome who was a witness to the assassination of Caesar. Write an account of this event and your reactions to it to a colleague holding government office in another Roman province.

2. Announce the death of Caesar to the world in a news report by means of satellite television communication. One member of your group should serve as a newsroom anchorperson, another as an on-site reporter. Include "live" interviews in your telecast. Compare your coverage of the event with the coverage by other "networks" (other groups).

3. What is going on in Antony's head when he is playing with the conspirators? Did he know what was happening already? Was he complicit? Does he have his own plans? How did he get there so quickly and know exactly how to act and what to do? Why was he so intent in making himself secure before making any commitment? Why was he allowed to make a funeral speech?

   As a reporter, you are going to ask these questions and get some answers for the viewers of tonight's news broadcast. Let's see how good a reporter you are when you role-play your interview for the rest of the class.

4. "I would like to know why all the senators fled the scene in such a great scramble? Were they afraid for their own lives or were they just the cowards that everyone saw them as? I would like to hear you, as a senator, speak about what happened at the Capitol that day."

   As the senator who is asked this question, prepare a speech in response to it and deliver it to the class. (You may have to watch a news channel or broadcast to get the drift of this one.)

5. Where were all of Caesar's supporters when the assassination happened? Did they all run off in terror or were they perhaps happy that the event occurred? You are a television reporter. Conduct street interviews asking this question of the Roman citizens to see what they think. Your interviews and the results you compile will be broadcast on the prime time news.

   You can set this activity up in any way that you think might work as long as you get enough information to make your broadcast viable and workable: you are the reporter.

6. Investigate the crime. As the tribune assigned to investigate Caesar's assassination, you decide to assemble as many clues as possible on a cork board or chalkboard so you can analyze how the pieces of information relate. Draw the crime scene and any clues you collected from it, and include representations of your suspects. You can use only the information you collect from interviews with citizens, senators, and any other witnesses that day. What motives can you find from the clues? How are the suspects related to the victim and to each other? Make connections wherever possible on your board. What is your reconstruction of this crime?

For the next scene ...

You have probably seen televised excerpts of the funeral of a famous person. In your journal describe what you remember about one or more of these grand events. What kind of funeral do you imagine for Julius Caesar?

Act 3, Scene 2

In this scene ...

Brutus and Cassius must now attempt to explain their actions to the people of Rome. They divide the crowd, and Cassius leaves with some of the citizens while Brutus remains on stage. He explains that his love of Rome is greater than his love for Caesar. Sudden death was the only way to liberate Rome from the threat of rule by a tyrant. He seems to succeed in convincing the people and departs, leaving Antony to conduct the funeral rites.

Mark Antony now delivers his speech. Appealing to the crowd's most basic instincts for tears, greed, and violence, he unleashes an outburst that results in civil revolt. The political and social order is destroyed. The horrors that he predicted in Scene 1 begin to take shape. The scene ends as the citizens carry Caesar's body to the burning funeral pyre. Flames from this pyre will be used not only to ignite the conspirators' houses but also to destroy the very foundations of the great Roman Empire.

11   *severally:* separately

13   *last:* the end of the speech
14   *lovers:* dear friends

17   *censure:* judge
18   *senses:* ability to understand

26   *fortunate:* successful

Scene 2

The Forum.
Enter Brutus and Cassius, and
a throng of Citizens.

Citizens: We will be satisfied; let us be satisfied.
Brutus: Then follow me, and give me audience, friends.
　Cassius, go you into the other street,
　And part the numbers.
　Those that will hear me speak, let 'em stay here;　　　5
　Those that will follow Cassius, go with him;
　And public reasons shall be rendered
　Of Cæsar's death.
First Citizen: I will hear Brutus speak.
Second Citizen: I will hear Cassius; and compare their
　　reasons,　　　　　　　　　　　　　　　　　　10
　When severally we hear them rendered.
　　　　　　[*Exit Cassius, with some of the Citizens.*
　　　　　　　　Brutus goes into the pulpit.]
Third Citizen: The noble Brutus is ascended: silence!
Brutus: Be patient till the last.
　Romans, countrymen, and lovers! hear me for my cause,
　and be silent, that you may hear: believe me for mine　15
　honour, and have respect to mine honour, that you
　may believe: censure me in your wisdom, and awake
　your senses, that you may the better judge. If there be
　any in this assembly, any dear friend of Cæsar's, to
　him I say, that Brutus' love to Cæsar was no less than　20
　his. If then that friend demand why Brutus rose
　against Cæsar, this is my answer: Not that I loved Cæsar
　less, but that I loved Rome more. Had you rather
　Cæsar were living and die all slaves, than that Cæsar
　were dead, to live all freemen? As Cæsar loved me,　25
　I weep for him; as he was fortunate, I rejoice at it;
　as he was valiant, I honour him: but, as he was
　ambitious, I slew him. There is tears for his love; joy

31   *bondman:* slave
32   *rude:* uncivilized

38   *question:* reason
39   *enrolled:* registered, recorded
40   *extenuated:* lessened, undervalued
41   *enforced:* exaggerated

44   *a place in the commonwealth:* a position of responsibility in the republic
46   *best lover:* closest friend

52   *parts:* qualities

59   *grace:* honour, respect
60   *Tending to:* relating to

for his fortune; honour for his valour; and death for
his ambition. Who is here so base that would be a   30
bondman? If any, speak; for him have I offended. Who
is here so rude that would not be a Roman? If any,
speak; for him have I offended. Who is here so vile that
will not love his country? If any, speak; for him have
I offended. I pause for a reply.   35
All: None, Brutus, none.
Brutus: Then none have I offended. I have done no more
to Cæsar than you shall do to Brutus. The question
of his death is enrolled in the Capitol; his glory not
extenuated, wherein he was worthy, nor his offences   40
enforced, for which he suffered death.

[*Enter Antony and others, with Cæsar's body.*]

Here comes his body, mourned by Mark Antony: who,
though he had no hand in his death, shall receive
the benefit of his dying, a place in the commonwealth;
as which of you shall not? With this I depart—that,   45
as I slew my best lover for the good of Rome, I have
the same dagger for myself, when it shall please my
country to need my death.
All: Live, Brutus! live, live!
First Citizen: Bring him with triumph home unto his house.   50
Second Citizen: Give him a statue with his ancestors.
Third Citizen: Let him be Cæsar.
Fourth Citizen: Cæsar's better parts
   Shall be crown'd in Brutus.
First Citizen: We'll bring him to his house with shouts and
   clamours.
Brutus: My countrymen——
Second Citizen: Peace! Silence! Brutus speaks.   55
First Citizen: Peace, ho!
Brutus: Good countrymen, let me depart alone,
   And, for my sake, stay here with Antony:
   Do grace to Cæsar's corpse, and grace his speech
   Tending to Cæsar's glories; which Mark Antony,   60
   By our permission, is allow'd to make.
   I do entreat you, not a man depart,
   Save I alone, till Antony have spoke.   [*Exit.*]

67   *beholding:* grateful, indebted

91   *ransoms:* payment made for the release of captured enemies; *general coffers:* public treasury

First Citizen: Stay, ho! and let us hear Mark Antony.
Third Citizen: Let him go up into the public chair; 65
    We'll hear him. Noble Antony, go up.
Antony: For Brutus' sake, I am beholding to you.
                              [*Goes into the pulpit.*]
Fourth Citizen: What does he say of Brutus?
Third Citizen: He says, for Brutus' sake
    He finds himself beholding to us all.
Fourth Citizen: 'Twere best he speak no harm of Brutus
    here. 70
First Citizen: This Cæsar was a tyrant.
Third Citizen: Nay, that's certain:
    We are blest that Rome is rid of him.
Second Citizen: Peace! Let us hear what Antony can say.
Antony: You gentle Romans——
Citizens: Peace, ho! let us hear him.
Antony: Friends, Romans, countrymen, lend me your ears; 75
    I come to bury Cæsar, not to praise him.
    The evil that men do lives after them;
    The good is oft interrèd with their bones;
    So let it be with Cæsar. The noble Brutus
    Hath told you Cæsar was ambitious: 80
    If it were so, it was a grievous fault,
    And grievously hath Cæsar answer'd it.
    Here, under leave of Brutus and the rest—
    For Brutus is an honourable man;
    So are they all, all honourable men— 85
    Come I to speak in Cæsar's funeral.
    He was my friend, faithful and just to me:
    But Brutus says he was ambitious;
    And Brutus is an honourable man.
    He hath brought many captives home to Rome, 90
    Whose ransoms did the general coffers fill:
    Did this in Cæsar seem ambitious?
    When that the poor hath cried, Cæsar hath wept:
    Ambition should be made of sterner stuff:
    Yet Brutus says he was ambitious; 95
    And Brutus is an honourable man.
    You all did see that on the Lupercal
    I thrice presented him a kingly crown,

112   *Caesar ... wrong:* Caesar has been unjustly treated.

116   *dear abide it:* pay a heavy price for it

122   *so poor:* so low in social status, so humble
123   *disposed:* inclined

132   *commons:* common people

Which he did thrice refuse: was this ambition?
Yet Brutus says he was ambitious;   100
And, sure, he is an honourable man.
I speak not to disprove what Brutus spoke,
But here I am to speak what I do know.
You all did love him once, not without cause:
What cause withholds you then to mourn for him?   105
O judgment! thou art fled to brutish beasts,
And men have lost their reason. Bear with me;
My heart is in the coffin there with Cæsar,
And I must pause till it come back to me.
First Citizen: Methinks there is much reason in his sayings.   110
Second Citizen: If thou consider rightly of the matter,
Cæsar has had great wrong.
Third Citizen: Has he, masters?
I fear there will a worse come in his place.
Fourth Citizen: Mark'd ye his words? He would not take
the crown;
Therefore 'tis certain he was not ambitious.   115
First Citizen: If it be found so, some will dear abide it.
Second Citizen: Poor soul! his eyes are red as fire with
weeping.
Third Citizen: There's not a nobler man in Rome than
Antony.
Fourth Citizen: Now mark him, he begins again to speak.
Antony: But yesterday the word of Cæsar might   120
Have stood against the world; now lies he there,
And none so poor to do him reverence.
O masters, if I were disposed to stir
Your hearts and minds to mutiny and rage,
I should do Brutus wrong, and Cassius wrong,   125
Who, you all know, are honourable men:
I will not do them wrong; I rather choose
To wrong the dead, to wrong myself and you,
Than I will wrong such honourable men.
But here's a parchment with the seal of Cæsar;   130
I found it in his closet, 'tis his will;
Let but the commons hear this testament—
Which, pardon me, I do not mean to read—
And they would go and kiss dead Cæsar's wounds

135   *napkins:* handkerchiefs

139   *issue:* children, descendants

143   *meet:* fitting

152   *o'ershot myself:* gone further than I intended

171   *mantle:* Caesar's toga

And dip their napkins in his sacred blood, 135
Yea, beg a hair of him for memory,
And, dying, mention it within their wills,
Bequeathing it as a rich legacy
Unto their issue.
Fourth Citizen: We'll hear the will: read it, Mark Antony. 140
All: The will! the will! we will hear Cæsar's will.
Antony: Have patience, gentle friends, I must not read it;
  It is not meet you know how Cæsar loved you.
  You are now wood, you are not stones, but men;
  And, being men, hearing the will of Cæsar, 145
  It will inflame you, it will make you mad:
  'Tis good you know not that you are his heirs;
  For, if you should, O, what would come of it!
Fourth Citizen: Read the will; we'll hear it, Antony;
  You shall read us the will, Cæsar's will. 150
Antony: Will you be patient? will you stay awhile?
  I have o'ershot myself to tell you of it:
  I fear I wrong the honourable men
  Whose daggers have stabb'd Cæsar; I do fear it.
Fourth Citizen: They were traitors: honourable men! 155
All: The will! the testament!
Second Citizen: They were villains, murderers: the will! read
    the will.
Antony: You will compel me then to read the will?
  Then make a ring about the corpse of Cæsar,
  And let me show you him that made the will. 160
  Shall I descend? and will you give me leave?
All: Come down.
Second Citizen: Descend.
                    [*He comes down from the pulpit.*]
Third Citizen: You shall have leave.
Fourth Citizen: A ring; stand round. 165
First Citizen: Stand from the hearse, stand from the body.
Second Citizen: Room for Antony, most noble Antony.
Antony: Nay, press not so upon me; stand far off.
Several Citizens: Stand back. Room! Bear back.
Antony: If you have tears, prepare to shed them now. 170
  You all do know this mantle: I remember
  The first time ever Cæsar put it on;

174   *Nervii:* the most warlike of the Gallic tribes. In 57 B.C.E.,
        Caesar fought courageously and overpowered this tribe.
        His victory was celebrated with great rejoicing.
176   *rent:* tear

180   *to be resolved:* to be assured

182   *Caesar's angel:* close friend of Caesar's

193   *flourish'd over:* triumphed over, overwhelmed

195   *dint:* force

197   *vesture:* garment, clothing
198   *marr'd:* mangled

'Twas on a summer's evening, in his tent,
That day he overcame the Nervii:
Look, in this place ran Cassius' dagger through: 175
See what a rent the envious Casca made:
Through this the well-beloved Brutus stabb'd;
And as he pluck'd his cursed steel away,
Mark how the blood of Cæsar follow'd it,
As rushing out of doors, to be resolved 180
If Brutus so unkindly knock'd, or no;
For Brutus, as you know, was Cæsar's angel:
Judge, O you gods, how dearly Cæsar loved him!
This was the most unkindest cut of all;
For when the noble Cæsar saw him stab, 185
Ingratitude, more strong than traitors' arms,
Quite vanquish'd him: then burst his mighty heart;
And, in his mantle muffling up his face,
Even at the base of Pompey's statue,
Which all the while ran blood, great Cæsar fell. 190
O, what a fall was there, my countrymen!
Then I, and you, and all of us fell down,
Whilst bloody treason flourish'd over us.
O, now you weep, and I perceive you feel
The dint of pity: these are gracious drops. 195
Kind souls, what weep you when you but behold
Our Cæsar's vesture wounded? Look you here,
Here is himself, marr'd, as you see, with traitors.
First Citizen: O piteous spectacle!
Second Citizen: O noble Cæsar! 200
Third Citizen: O woeful day!
Fourth Citizen: O traitors, villains!
First Citizen: O most bloody sight!
Second Citizen: We will be revenged.
All: Revenge! About! Seek! Burn! Fire! Kill! Slay! Let not
    a traitor live! 205
Antony: Stay, countrymen.
First Citizen: Peace there! hear the noble Antony.
Second Citizen: We'll hear him, we'll follow him, we'll die
    with him.
Antony: Good friends, sweet friends let me not stir you up
    To such a sudden flood of mutiny. 210

212   *private griefs:* personal complaints or causes

219   *public leave:* permission to speak in public

221–222 *Action:* gestures; *nor the power ... men's blood:* the ability
         to persuade people by forceful argument and delivery; the
         power to excite people to action
222   *right on:* directly

227   *ruffle up:* enrage, incite to riot

248   *arbours:* gardens

They that have done this deed are honourable:
What private griefs they have, alas, I know not,
That made them do it: they are wise and honourable,
And will, no doubt, with reasons answer you.
I come not, friends, to steal away your hearts: 215
I am no orator, as Brutus is;
But, as you know me all, a plain blunt man,
That love my friend; and that they know full well
That gave me public leave to speak of him:
For I have neither wit, nor words, nor worth, 220
Action, nor utterance, nor the power of speech,
To stir men's blood: I only speak right on;
I tell you that which you yourselves do know;
Show you sweet Cæsar's wounds, poor poor dumb
      mouths,
And bid them speak for me: but were I Brutus, 225
And Brutus Antony, there were an Antony
Would ruffle up your spirits, and put a tongue
In every wound of Cæsar, that should move
The stones of Rome to rise and mutiny.
All: We'll mutiny. 230
First Citizen: We'll burn the house of Brutus.
Third Citizen: Away, then! come, seek the conspirators.
Antony: Yet hear me, countrymen; yet hear me speak.
All: Peace, ho! Hear Antony. Most noble Antony!
Antony: Why, friends, you go to do you know not what: 235
    Wherein hath Cæsar thus deserved your loves?
    Alas, you know not: I must tell you then:
    You have forgot the will I told you of.
All: Most true: the will! Let's stay and hear the will.
Antony: Here is the will, and under Cæsar's seal. 240
    To every Roman citizen he gives,
    To every several man, seventy-five drachmas.
Second Citizen: Most noble Cæsar! We'll revenge his death.
Third Citizen: O royal Cæsar!
Antony: Hear me with patience. 245
All: Peace, ho!
Antony: Moreover, he hath left you all his walks,
    His private arbours and new-planted orchards,
    On this side Tiber; he hath left them you,

254   *the holy place:* the part of the Forum where bodies were cremated
255   *brands:* pieces of burning wood

266   *upon a wish:* just as I had hoped; *Fortune:* the goddess of fate

269   *Are rid like madmen:* They were seen on horseback fleeing the Roman mobs.
270   *Belike ... the people:* It is likely that they received news of the anger of the people following the assassination and Antony's speech.

And to your heirs for ever; common pleasures,   250
  To walk abroad and recreate yourselves.
  Here was a Cæsar! when comes such another?
First Citizen: Never, never. Come, away, away!
  We'll burn his body in the holy place,
  And with the brands fire the traitors' houses.   255
  Take up the body.
Second Citizen: Go fetch fire.
Third Citizen: Pluck down benches.
Fourth Citizen: Pluck down forms, windows, anything.
                     [Exeunt Citizens with the body.]
Antony: Now let it work. Mischief, thou art afoot,   260
  Take thou what course thou wilt!

[*Enter a Servant.*]

                    How now, fellow!
Servant: Sir, Octavius is already come to Rome.
Antony: Where is he?
Servant: He and Lepidus are at Cæsar's house.
Antony: And thither will I straight to visit him: 265
  He comes upon a wish. Fortune is merry,
  And in this mood will give us anything.
Servant: I heard him say, Brutus and Cassius
  Are rid like madmen through the gates of Rome.
Antony: Belike they had some notice of the people,   270
  How I had moved them. Bring me to Octavius.
                      [Exeunt.]

Act 3, Scene 2: Activities

1. After reading and/or listening several times to Brutus's speech and Antony's speech to the citizens, write down your responses to each one. You may wish to use the following questions to help you organize your comments:

   • For what reason does each speaker address the crowd?
   • What feelings did you experience as you read and/or heard each speech?
   • What effect does each speech have on Brutus's and Antony's audience?
   • What is there about the way each speech is written and presented that accounts for this effect? Consider elements such as the following: idea content, language, length, and audience participation.

   Discuss your written responses with others in your group. Write a summary of the group's feelings about each speech, assessing the overall effectiveness of each delivery.

2. This is the scene of persuasive speeches. Both Brutus and Cassius are supposed to address the populace of Rome, but we see and hear only Brutus's speech. We know that Cassius is a persuasive person, so write the speech that he probably gave but that Shakespeare didn't include in the play. Deliver your speech to the class.

   As class members, decide what effect you think this speech had on the audience who heard it. Compare Cassius's speech to that given by Brutus. Why do you think Shakespeare never included this powerful speech in the play? Record your observations and conclusions in your response journal.

3. Oratory (the art of skillful public speaking) is a tremendously useful tool in terms of success in business. Abraham Lincoln gave an address at Gettysburg in November 1863 that lasted less than two minutes. The other speaker, a successful orator named Edward Everett,

waxed on for hours but nobody remembers him or what he said, while everybody knows about Lincoln's speech. Why was one speech effective and the other one wasn't? To figure this out will require some research. Incidentally, the press at the time thought that Everett's speech was worth reporting but that Lincoln's wasn't.

Brutus gave a speech similar to Lincoln's. Why didn't Brutus's work when Lincoln's did? In your groups, decide why everyone quotes from Antony's speech and not from Brutus's? Make a journal record of your conclusions.

Examine Lincoln's Gettysburg speech and Brutus's speech. Write a short, expository essay in which you address the topic of effective speech making as a tool for success and suggest in it why Antony succeeded when Brutus failed.

4. You are a Roman centurion (a police officer) on crowd-control duty. It is your job to make sure that the crowd attending the public funeral for Caesar is orderly and doesn't degenerate into an uncontrollable mob. It does, however, and you have to make a detailed report to your superiors about what went wrong, what you did, and why you did it. Write that report.

5. Draw a picture that you think best illustrates the events in this scene. Include a description of why you drew what you did and what it might mean in terms of the action of the play so far. In your journal, decide for yourself if the drawing is as effective as an essay description of those events.

For the next scene ...

Crowd control at major events is a significant issue today, and there are many suggestions as to how it should be dealt with. What are your views? What do you think are the motivations behind a peaceful crowd becoming a mob? What is the danger of mobs anyway? How would you, as a politician, deal with a "mob problem"?

Act 3, Scene 3

In this scene ...

Cinna the poet appears on a street near the Forum. He speaks of a threatening dream and expresses fears of what may happen to him. A band of unruly citizens arrives. They mistakenly believe that he is Cinna the conspirator. Even after they realize their mistake, they senselessly slay him and continue on a rampage of violence and destruction through the city streets.

2 *And things ... fantasy:* Events give a terrible significance to what I have been dreaming or imagining. *charge:* fill; *fantasy:* imaginings

18 *bear me a bang:* receive a blow from me

27 *Cinna:* Helvius Cinna, the poet. The historian Plutarch records that the rioting citizens mistook him for Cinna the conspirator and killed him.

Scene 3

The same. A street.
Enter Cinna the poet.

Cinna: I dreamt to-night that I did feast with Cæsar,
  And things unluckily charge my fantasy:
  I have no will to wander forth of doors,
  Yet something leads me forth.

  [*Enter Citizens.*]

First Citizen: What is your name?   5
Second Citizen: Whither are you going?
Third Citizen: Where do you dwell?
Fourth Citizen: Are you a married man or a bachelor?
Second Citizen: Answer every man directly.
First Citizen: Ay, and briefly.   10
Fourth Citizen: Ay, and wisely.
Third Citizen: Ay, and truly, you were best.
Cinna: What is my name? Whither am I going? Where do I
    dwell? Am I a married man or a bachelor? Then, to
    answer every man directly and briefly, wisely and   15
    truly: wisely I say, I am a bachelor.
Second Citizen: That's as much as to say, they are fools that
    marry: you'll bear me a bang for that, I fear. Proceed;
    directly.
Cinna: Directly, I am going to Cæsar's funeral.   20
First Citizen: As a friend or an enemy?
Cinna: As a friend.
Second Citizen: That matter is answered directly.
Fourth Citizen: For your dwelling, briefly.
Cinna: Briefly, I dwell by the Capitol.   25
Third Citizen: Your name, sir, truly.
Cinna: Truly, my name is Cinna.
First Citizen: Tear him to pieces; he's a conspirator.

33–34   *pluck ... going:* Simply tear his name out of his heart and let
          him go.

Cinna: I am Cinna the poet, I am Cinna the poet.
Fourth Citizen: Tear him for his bad verses, tear him for   30
    his bad verses.
Cinna: I am not Cinna the conspirator.
Fourth Citizen: It is no matter, his name's Cinna; pluck but
    his name out of his heart, and turn him going.
Third Citizen: Tear him, tear him! Come brands, ho!   35
    firebrands: to Brutus', to Cassius'; burn all: some
    to Decius' house, and some to Casca's; some to
    Ligarius': away, go!   [*Exeunt.*]

Act 3, Scene 3: Activities

1. To many people, this scene seems to serve no logical function in the play at all. As a theatre or film director, indicate to your cast why it *is* necessary and what issues it highlights. You might wish to refer as far back as Act 1, Scene 1, when giving your explanation. Write out your directive so that your rationale is very clear, and present it to the class for their comments.

2. For many viewers, this is a truly frightening scene. With your group, discuss what aspects of it make you uncomfortable. In your journal, record an incident that you have experienced or that you know about, similar to the mob scene depicted here. What was the ultimate result of the incident?

3. Write a newspaper feature on the attack on Cinna the poet. In your account, try to include the following:

   - how and why the crowd were provoked to attack Cinna
   - how Cinna might have avoided the confrontation
   - why nobody could control the crowd
   - how the crowd took the law in their own hands to avenge the murder of Caesar

   In your feature story, include your opinion on crowd violence. Comment too on whether you think Mark Antony had anything to do with promoting Cinna's untimely death and whether you think Cinna deserved what happened to him.

Act 3: Consider the Whole Act

1. In this act, Cinna the poet speaks of discomforting dreams. We remember Calpurnia's dream in Act 2. Invent a dream that Antony might tell about. To help you, consult your journal entries on your impression of him and recall events of the scenes in which he participates. Write a speech for Antony in which he describes his dream to Octavius.

2. Explore some of the historical records and accounts of the assassination of Julius Caesar on the Ides of March to discover the similarities and some of the differences between the real event in history and Shakespeare's dramatic account of the event.

   Prepare a written and/or audio-visual summary of your findings and conclusions at the end of the time period specified for this activity.

3. Study political cartoons, in newspapers and magazines, that give humorous dramatic expression to political figures and political issues of today.

   With a partner, decide which character or event from Act 3 could be captured in a political cartoon. Draw or write a description of the character/situation you have chosen to portray humorously.

   If you have created a visual representation, provide an appropriate caption for it.

4. The assassination of Julius Caesar is a major news event in Rome, and all the media are scrambling to report it in as much detail as they can. As a journalist, create your version of the story as you understand it for a television special report or for a front page story in a newspaper.

5. Both Portia and Calpurnia are women of significant power and stature in the play. Compare them in terms of their roles in their respective marriages, the influence they have over their husbands, and the influence they might have had in the outcome of the play so far. Decide why they were not as effective as they might have been. You might wish to extend this activity to include the role of women generally in both Roman and Elizabethan society.

6. Design four of the costumes for characters in the play using Roman, Elizabethan, or modern dress. Research possible designs to authenticate them. Draw your costumes in colour and indicate the scenes for which they are intended. Display your costume designs for the class.

7. With your group, record some examples of times when you yourself, someone in history or contemporary life, or a fictional character has had to choose between honour and ambition. What choices had to be made? What were the consequences of these choices? What might have happened had an alternative course of action been chosen? Relate the discoveries you have made here to the play and prepare an essay on the conflict between ambition and honour.

8. The scene involving Cinna the poet points out the confusion that often surrounds names. In this case, the consequences are terrible indeed. Suggest in an essay how this brief scene highlights a main theme about the confusion among names throughout the play.

For the next scene ...

Think of places you know where large-scale civil disobedience and social violence have occurred. Some examples from history are the French Revolution, the American Revolution, the expulsion of the British from countries such as India and South Africa.

In what other places have people fought for political change? How was order restored? Did the restoration of order end the problems that had created the disobedience and violence?

What experiences have people you know or know about had when they fought a government system?

Act 4, Scene 1

In this scene ...

This scene takes place some months later in Antony's house. The self-appointed group of three who now rule Rome and Italy—Antony, Octavius, and Lepidus—are concluding a meeting. As the scene begins, they are drawing up a list of names of people whom they intend to put to death. Antony sends Lepidus to Caesar's house to obtain the will so they can change its terms to suit their own purposes. As soon as Lepidus departs, Antony openly reveals his true opinion of the man.

In the closing lines of the scene, Antony reports that Brutus and Cassius are recruiting armies. Both Antony and Octavius must now make careful plans to overcome the dangers that threaten their rule.

1   *prick'd:* marked (with a pinprick on the list). In Roman times, names were written on wax tablets and thus were checked off by pricking the wax beside the name.

6   *with a spot ... him:* With a mark beside his name, I condemn him.

9   *cut off ... legacies:* alter the will by reducing the bequests or eliminating some of the heirs

14   *The threefold world divided:* The Roman Empire was divided into three parts: Europe, Asia, and Africa. After Caesar's death, Octavius, Antony, and Lepidus ruled these areas as the Second Triumvirate.

17   *proscription:* condemnation to die

20   *To ... slanderous loads:* to take away some of the suspicion (blame) from ourselves

27   *in commons:* in public pastures

Act 4, Scene 1

A house in Rome.
Antony, Octavius, and Lepidus,
seated at a table.

Antony: These many, then, shall die: their names are prick'd.
Octavius: Your brother too must die; consent you, Lepidus?
Lepidus: I do consent——
Octavius: Prick him down, Antony.
Lepidus: Upon condition Publius shall not live,
   Who is your sister's son, Mark Antony.   5
Antony: He shall not live; look, with a spot I damn him.
   But, Lepidus, go you to Cæsar's house,
   Fetch the will hither, and we shall determine
   How to cut off some charge in legacies.
Lepidus: What, shall I find you here?   10
Octavius: Or here, or at the Capitol.   [*Exit Lepidus.*]
Antony: This is a slight unmeritable man,
   Meet to be sent on errands: is it fit,
   The threefold world divided, he should stand
   One of the three to share it?
Octavius: So you thought him,   15
   And took his voice who should be prick'd to die,
   In our black sentence and proscription.
Antony: Octavius, I have seen more days than you:
   And though we lay these honours on this man,
   To ease ourselves of divers slanderous loads,   20
   He shall but bear them as the ass bears gold,
   To groan and sweat under the business,
   Either led or driven, as we point the way;
   And having brought our treasure where we will
   Then take we down his load and turn him off   25
   Like to the empty ass, to shake his ears,
   And graze in commons.

30	*appoint ... provender:* assign him a supply of food
32	*to wind:* to turn
33	*corporal:* physical; *spirit:* mind
34	*in some taste ... but so:* In some respects Lepidus is the same.
36	*barren-spirited:* without initiative or original ideas of his own
37	*abjects:* things that have been thrown away because they are of no value; *orts:* leftovers or scraps. The reference is to Lepidus's inadequate or second-rate characteristics as a leader.
39	*Begin his fashion:* are new to him
42	*levying powers:* raising military forces

46	*covert:* hidden
47	*surest answered:* most effectively dealt with
48–49	*for ... enemies:* a reference to the Elizabethan fascination with bear-baiting: a practice in which a bear was tied to a stake and dogs were released to attack it. Bets were taken on the outcome. The bear never won.

Octavius: You may do your will;
   But he's a tried and valiant soldier.
Antony: So is my horse, Octavius; and for that
   I do appoint him store of provender: 30
   It is a creature that I teach to fight,
   To wind, to stop, to run directly on,
   His corporal motion govern'd by my spirit.
   And, in some taste, is Lepidus but so;
   He must be taught, and train'd, and bid go forth;   35
   A barren-spirited fellow; one that feeds
   On abjects, orts, and imitations,
   Which, out of use and staled by other men,
   Begin his fashion: do not talk of him
   But as a property. And now, Octavius,   40
   Listen great things: Brutus and Cassius
   Are levying powers: we must straight make head;
   Therefore let our alliance be combined,
   Our best friends made, our means stretch'd;
   And let us presently go sit in council,   45
   How covert matters may be best disclosed,
   And open perils surest answered.
Octavius: Let us do so: for we are at the stake
   And bay'd about with many enemies;
   And some that smile have in their hearts, I fear,   50
   Millions of mischiefs.   [*Exeunt.*]

Act 4, Scene 1: Activities

1. As this scene opens, Antony, Octavius, and Lepidus are concluding a meeting that has been going on for some time.

   a) Write an account of what may have been discussed earlier in the meeting. Compare your version with those of others in your group.
   b) Prepare what could have been the agenda for the meeting and a summary of the decisions made during the meeting.
   c) Decide what you think each of the three members of the triumvirate will do at the end of the meeting.

   In your journal, make a note of your impressions of Antony, Octavius, and Lepidus from this scene.

2. What does Antony's plan to discard Lepidus suggest to you about the nature of political power sharing?

   What example(s) of twentieth century political organizations can you think of where one branch or section has taken an action without listening to the advisory branch of the organization?

   In an organization of which you have been a member, what has happened when one member of the executive refuses to share information with the others?

   Discuss your experience and observations with others. Decide what qualities you think are necessary for people to share leadership effectively.

3. As a political commentator, prepare a paper for broadcast (one or two minutes in length) in which you comment on the preparations Antony and Octavius are making to defeat the opposing forces, the challenge they face, and your sense of what it is they hope to achieve.

   Present your political commentary to an audience.

4. As Brutus, you have just received the news that one hundred senators have been "proscribed" (denounced and condemned as being dangerous to the state). Write letters to both Antony and Octavius expressing your concerns about the actions they have taken.

5. This is our first look at Octavius in action and we learn something about him. Record your impressions of this man, indicating the traits of character that might make him as important and powerful a leader as Caesar himself. This could take the form of a biographical article or a profile in a television newscast or in an important weekend newspaper feature.

For the next scene ...

Recall a situation in which a plan or important project that you and your group undertook did not turn out as you had hoped. How did you react? How did the others react? What did you decide to do?

Act 4, Scene 2

In this scene ...

Two years have passed since Caesar's assassination. Brutus's army has set up camp in the hills of Sardis in Asia Minor. Brutus, accompanied by his officers and his boy servant, Lucius, arrives before his tent. The news that Cassius has also arrived with his army is announced. Brutus criticizes Cassius in front of Cassius's servant, Pindarus, and again in front of his own officer, Lucilius. Cassius arrives and he and Brutus meet for the first time in several months. After a brief but tense exchange, Brutus invites Cassius into his tent to discuss privately their mutual concerns.

7   *ill officers:* bad subordinate officers

16   *familiar instances:* friendly greetings
17   *conference:* discussion

21   *enforced ceremony:* artificial or strained courtesy

23   *horses hot at hand:* spirited horses held tightly in rein

Scene 2

*Camp near Sardis. Before
Brutus' tent.*

*Drum. Enter Brutus, Lucilius,
Lucius, and Soldiers; Titinius and
Pindarus meeting them.*

Brutus: Stand, ho!
Lucilius: Give the word, ho! and stand.
Brutus: What now, Lucilius! is Cassius near?
Lucilius: He is at hand; and Pindarus is come
   To do your salutation from his master.   5
Brutus: He greets me well. Your master, Pindarus,
   In his own charge, or by ill officers,
   Hath given me some worthy cause to wish
   Things done, undone: but if he be at hand,
   I shall be satisfied.
Pindarus: I do not doubt   10
   But that my noble master will appear
   Such as he is, full of regard and honour.
Brutus: He is not doubted. A word, Lucilius,
   How he received you: let me be resolved.
Lucilius: With courtesy and with respect enough;   15
   But not with such familiar instances,
   Nor with such free and friendly conference,
   As he hath used of old.
Brutus: Thou hast described
   A hot friend cooling: ever note, Lucilius,
   When love begins to sicken and decay,   20
   It useth an enforced ceremony.
   There are no tricks in plain and simple faith;
   But hollow men, like horses hot at hand,
   Make gallant show and promise of their mettle;
   But when they should endure the bloody spur,   25

26   *fall their crests:* droop their necks; *deceitful jades:* horses that seemed energetic and spirited but that were in reality worn out

28   *Sardis:* the capital of the region of Lydia in Asia Minor, a peninsula between the Black Sea and the Mediterranean, which includes most of what is now Asiatic Turkey

29   *the horse in general:* the cavalry

31   *gently:* slowly and steadily

41   *be content:* control yourself, be calm

42   *griefs:* grievances, complaints against

46   *enlarge your griefs:* discuss your complaints in greater detail

48   *charges:* troops

They fall their crests, and, like deceitful jades,
   Sink in the trial. Comes his army on?
Lucilius: They mean this night in Sardis to be quarter'd;
   The greater part, the horse in general,
   Are come with Cassius.   [Low march within.]
Brutus: Hark! he is arrived.   30
   March gently on to meet him.

[Enter Cassius and his powers.]

Cassius: Stand, ho!
Brutus: Stand, ho! Speak the word along.
First Soldier: Stand!
Second Soldier: Stand!   35
Third Soldier: Stand!
Cassius: Most noble brother, you have done me wrong.
Brutus: Judge me, you gods! wrong I mine enemies?
   And, if not so, how should I wrong a brother?
Cassius: Brutus, this sober form of yours hides wrongs;   40
   And when you do them——
Brutus: Cassius, be content;
   Speak your griefs softly: I do know you well.
   Before the eyes of both our armies here,
   Which should perceive nothing but love from us,
   Let us not wrangle: bid them move away;   45
   Then in my tent, Cassius, enlarge your griefs,
   And I will give you audience.
Cassius: Pindarus,
   Bid our commanders lead their charges off
   A little from this ground.
Brutus: Lucilius, do you the like; and let no man   50
   Come to our tent till we have done our conference.
   Lucius and Titinius guard our door.   [Exeunt.]

Act 4, Scene 2: Activities

1. This is the first time that we have seen Brutus and Cassius since they were forced to flee Rome. What do you think has been happening to these two leaders since their departure?

   In groups, write two or three diary entries or letters that either Cassius or Brutus could have written in their time away from each other. One group could write the entries for Cassius, while the other group prepares Brutus's entries.

   Exchange entries and discuss your responses to them.

2. References to animals occur frequently in literature. Recall the images of a horse that appear in both Scenes 1 and 2 of this act. What are the horses compared to in these scenes? Do you find the comparisons effective? Why or why not?

   Begin recording other references to animals that appear throughout the rest of the play.

   At the end of the play, discuss other animal references you noted and your responses to them.

For the next scene ...

What kinds of problems or situations can develop between close friends to strain their relationship? Why does a true friendship usually survive the difficulties that may threaten it?

Act 4, Scene 3

In this scene ...

Inside the tent Brutus and Cassius begin to quarrel.
They exchange accusations and bitter insults as the
conflict becomes more and more heated. Finally,
however, the two friends become reconciled. A poet
enters and attempts to keep the two generals from
fighting. Cassius laughs at the shallow man, but Brutus
orders him removed. After calm has been restored,
Brutus confides to Cassius that his wife, Portia, has
killed herself.

The two commanders, Titinius and Messala, arrive.
They report that Octavius and Antony are leading their
armies to Philippi. Brutus suggests that he and Cassius
go forth to meet their enemies. Cassius cautions Brutus
not to march but rather to wait for their enemies to
attack. Brutus overrules Cassius and decides to lead
the armies into battle, departing early in the morning.
Cassius and the others leave.

While his company sleeps, the restless Brutus reads.
From out of the darkness, the ghost of Caesar appears
to him. He announces that he shall see Brutus at
Philippi. When the apparition has dissolved, Brutus
awakens his officers who say they have seen nothing.
Making his decision quickly, Brutus gives orders to
begin the march at once.

2   *noted:* publicly disgraced

4   *praying on his side:* speaking on his behalf, defending him
5   *slighted off:* disregarded

8   *nice:* trivial, insignificant

10   *much condemn'd:* often accused
11   *mart ... gold:* market official positions like merchandise

15   *honours:* gives respectability to

21   *And not:* except

23   *supporting robbers:* apparently a newly identified charge
      against Caesar—of protecting dishonest politicians or
      officials—but one that must have been previously
      considered by the conspirators
25   *mighty ... honours:* the great opportunities to continue being
      honourable and honoured
26   *may be grasped thus:* easily acquired
27   *bay:* howl at

Scene 3

Brutus' tent.

Enter Brutus and Cassius.

Cassius: That you have wrong'd me doth appear in this:
 You have condemn'd and noted Lucius Pella
 For taking bribes here of the Sardians;
 Wherein my letters, praying on his side,
 Because I knew the man, were slighted off.   5
Brutus: You wrong'd yourself to write in such a case.
Cassius: In such a time as this it is not meet
 That every nice offence should bear his comment.
Brutus: Let me tell you, Cassius, you yourself
 Are much condemn'd to have an itching palm; 10
 To sell and mart your offices for gold
 To undeservers.
Cassius: I an itching palm?
 You know that you are Brutus that speaks this,
 Or, by the gods, this speech were else your last.
Brutus: The name of Cassius honours this corruption. 15
 And chastisement doth therefore hide his head.
Cassius: Chastisement!
Brutus: Remember March, the Ides of March remember:
 Did not great Julius bleed for justice' sake?
 What villain touch'd his body, that did stab, 20
 And not for justice? What, shall one of us,
 That struck the foremost man of all this world
 But for supporting robbers, shall we now
 Contaminate our fingers with base bribes,
 And sell the mighty space of our large honours 25
 For so much trash as may be grasped thus?
 I had rather be a dog, and bay the moon,
 Than such a Roman.

30   *To hedge me in:* to limit me; restrict my possible courses of action

39   *choler:* anger, temper

44   *budge:* give in
45   *observe:* pay attention to

47   *spleen:* anger. In Shakespeare's time the spleen was thought to be the bodily source of emotions.

50   *waspish:* bad-tempered

52   *vaunting:* boasting

54   *learn of:* learn from

58   *moved:* angered
59   *tempted:* provoked

Cassius: Brutus, bay not me;
  I'll not endure it: you forget yourself,
  To hedge me in; I am a soldier, I,   30
  Older in practice, abler than yourself
  To make conditions.
Brutus: Go to; you are not Cassius.
Cassius: I am.
Brutus: I say you are not.
Cassius: Urge me no more, I shall forget myself;   35
  Have mind upon your health, tempt me no further.
Brutus: Away, slight man!
Cassius: Is't possible?
Brutus: Hear me, for I will speak.
  Must I give way and room to your rash choler?
  Shall I be frighted when a madman stares?   40
Cassius: O ye gods, ye gods! must I endure all this?
Brutus: All this! ay, more: fret till your proud heart break;
  Go show your slaves how choleric you are,
  And make your bondmen tremble. Must I budge,
  Must I observe you? Must I stand and crouch   45
  Under your testy humour? By the gods,
  You shall digest the venom of your spleen,
  Though it do split you; for, from this day forth,
  I'll use you for my mirth, yea, for my laughter,
  When you are waspish.
Cassius: Is it come to this?   50
Brutus: You say you are a better soldier:
  Let it appear so; make your vaunting true,
  And it shall please me well: for mine own part,
  I shall be glad to learn of noble men.
Cassius: You wrong me every way; you wrong me, Brutus; 55
  I said, an elder soldier, not a better:
  Did I say better?
Brutus: If you did, I care not.
Cassius: When Cæsar lived, he durst not thus have
    moved me.
Brutus: Peace, peace! you durst not so have tempted him.
Cassius: I durst not!   60
Brutus: No.
Cassius: What, durst not tempt him!

72   *coin my heart:* sell my heart for money

75   *indirection:* dishonesty
76   *to pay my legions:* Roman soldiers were directly employed
          and paid by their generals, not by the state. Therefore, a
          constant supply of money was needed and failure to pay
          one's soldiers resulted in their desertion—usually to a
          general who could pay them.

80   *rascal counters:* worthless coins, used only for counting

84   *rived:* torn apart, broken

95   *braved:* defied
96   *Check'd:* corrected
97   *conn'd by rote:* learned by heart

Brutus: For your life you durst not.
Cassius: Do not presume too much upon my love;
    I may do that I shall be sorry for.
Brutus: You have done that you should be sorry for.   65
    There is no terror, Cassius, in your threats;
    For I am arm'd so strong in honesty
    That they pass by me as the idle wind,
    Which I respect not. I did send to you
    For certain sums of gold, which you denied me: 70
    For I can raise no money by vile means:
    By heaven, I had rather coin my heart,
    And drop my blood for drachmas, than to wring
    From the hard hands of peasants their vile trash
    By any indirection: I did send   75
    To you for gold to pay my legions,
    Which you denied me: was that done like Cassius?
    Should I have answer'd Caius Cassius so?
    When Marcus Brutus grows so covetous,
    To lock such rascal counters from his friends,   80
    Be ready, gods, with all your thunderbolts,
    Dash him to pieces!
Cassius: I denied you not.
Brutus: You did.
Cassius: I did not: he was but a fool
    That brought my answer back. Brutus hath
      rived my heart:
    A friend should bear his friend's infirmities,   85
    But Brutus makes mine greater than they are.
Brutus: I do not, till you practise them on me.
Cassius: You love me not.
Brutus: I do not like your faults.
Cassius: A friendly eye could never see such faults.
Brutus: A flatterer's would not, though they do appear   90
    As huge as high Olympus.
Cassius: Come, Antony, and young Octavius, come,
    Revenge yourselves alone on Cassius,
    For Cassius is aweary of the world;
    Hated by one he loves; braved by his brother;   95
    Check'd like a bondman; all his faults observed,
    Set in a note-book, learn'd, and conn'd by rote,

98   *To cast into my teeth:* to throw in my face

101   *Plutus:* the god of riches

108   *dishonour shall be humour:* I shall consider your insults to me as a fit of bad temper or an impulse.

111   *much enforced:* struck strongly and repeatedly

To cast into my teeth. O, I could weep
My spirit from mine eyes! There is my dagger,
And here my naked breast; within, a heart   100
Dearer than Plutus' mine, richer than gold:
If that thou be'st a Roman, take it forth;
I, that denied thee gold, will give my heart:
Strike, as thou didst at Cæsar; for I know,
When thou didst hate him worst, thou lovedst him better   105
Than ever thou lovedst Cassius.
Brutus: Sheathe your dagger:
Be angry when you will, it shall have scope;
Do what you will, dishonour shall be humour.
O Cassius, you are yoked with a lamb
That carries anger as the flint bears fire,   110
Who, much enforced, shows a hasty spark
And straight is cold again.
Cassius: Hath Cassius lived
To be but mirth and laughter to his Brutus,
When grief and blood ill-temper'd vexeth him?
Brutus: When I spoke that, I was ill-temper'd too.   115
Cassius: Do you confess so much? Give me your hand.
Brutus: And my heart too.
Cassius: O Brutus!
Brutus: What's the matter?
Cassius: Have not you love enough to bear with me,
When that rash humour which my mother gave me
Makes me forgetful?
Brutus: Yes, Cassius, and from henceforth,   120
When you are over-earnest with your Brutus,
He'll think your mother chides, and leave you so.
Poet [Within]: Let me go in to see the generals;
There is some grudge between 'em; 'tis not meet
They be alone.   125
Lucilius [Within]: You shall not come to them.
Poet [Within]: Nothing but death shall stay me.

[*Enter Poet, followed by Lucilius, Titinius, and Lucius.*]

Cassius: How now! what's the matter?
Poet: For shame, you generals! what do you mean?
Love, and be friends, as two such men should be;   130

132   *cynic:* rude person

135   *his time:* the proper or suitable time
136   *jigging fools:* writers of foolish and meaningless verses

144   *Of your philosophy ... use:* You are not being very philosophical if you give in to difficulties that only happen by chance. Brutus followed the philosophy of Stoicism, which held that natural events were not chance but the expressions of the power of a wise and good god. Pain and suffering were not evil but natural and were therefore to be endured. Happiness was not necessary; it was duty, fortitude, and self-control that were important.

145   *accidental evils:* bad luck over which people have no control

154   *fell distract:* became depressed and went out of her mind
155   *swallow'd fire:* Plutarch, a Greek biographer and writer of the time, indicates Portia asphyxiated herself by filling her mouth with hot coals; others suggest "swallowing fire" means taking poison.

For I have seen more years, I'm sure, than ye.
Cassius: Ha, ha! how vilely doth this cynic rhyme!
Brutus: Get you hence, sirrah; saucy fellow, hence!
Cassius: Bear with him, Brutus; 'tis his fashion.
Brutus: I'll know his humour, when he knows his time.   135
    What should the wars do with these jigging fools?
    Companion, hence!
Cassius: Away, away, be gone!
                                [*Exit Poet.*]
Brutus: Lucilius and Titinius, bid the commanders
    Prepare to lodge their companies to-night.
Cassius: And come yourselves, and bring Messala with you   140
    Immediately to us.   [*Exeunt Lucilius and Titinius.*]
Brutus: Lucius, a bowl of wine! [*Exit Lucius.*]
Cassius: I did not think you could have been so angry.
Brutus: O Cassius, I am sick of many griefs.
Cassius: Of your philosophy you make no use,
    If you give place to accidental evils.   145
Brutus: No man bears sorrow better. Portia is dead.
Cassius: Ha! Portia!
Brutus: She is dead.
Cassius: How 'scaped I killing when I cross'd you so?
    O insupportable and touching loss!   150
    Upon what sickness?
Brutus: Impatient of my absence,
    And grief that young Octavius with Mark Antony
    Have made themselves so strong: for with her death
    That tidings came: with this she fell distract,
    And, her attendants absent, swallow'd fire.   155
Cassius: And died so?
Brutus: Even so.
Cassius: O ye immortal gods!

[*Re-enter Lucius, with wine and taper.*]

Brutus: Speak no more of her. Give me a bowl of wine.
    In this I bury all unkindness, Cassius.   [*Drinks.*]
Cassius: My heart is thirsty for that noble pledge.
    Fill, Lucius, till the wine o'erswell the cup;   160
    I cannot drink too much of Brutus' love.   [*Drinks.*]
                          [*Exit Lucius.*]

164   *call in question:* closely examine, carefully consider

169   *Bending their expedition:* directing their movement or march
170   *tenour:* meaning

172   *proscription:* an announcement or declaration condemning someone to death; *bills of outlawry:* lists of those people who have been sentenced to death

188   *she is dead:* Brutus has already discussed Portia's death with Cassius (line 146) and yet is apparently hearing about it here for the first time from Messala. There are two theories about this duplication. Some Shakespearean scholars believe that when Shakespeare rewrote this scene, he inserted a second version (line 146) and that both versions were left in by mistake (by Shakespeare, the editor, or the printer). Other scholars think that Shakespeare intended to include both versions and that when Brutus hears about his wife's death from Messala, he is using the opportunity to reinforce his image as a Stoic.

193   *in art:* in theory or in knowledge, if not in experience

[*Re-enter Titinius, with Messala.*]

Brutus: Come in, Titinius! Welcome, good Messala.
　Now sit we close about this taper here,
　And call in question our necessities.
Cassius: Portia, art thou gone?
Brutus: 　　　　　　　　No more, I pray you.　　165
　Messala, I have here received letters,
　That young Octavius and Mark Antony
　Come down upon us with a mighty power,
　Bending their expedition towards Philippi.
Messala: Myself have letters of the selfsame tenour.　　170
Brutus: With what addition?
Messala: That by proscription and bills of outlawry,
　Octavius, Antony, and Lepidus,
　Have put to death an hundred senators.
Brutus: Therein our letters do not well agree;　　175
　Mine speak of seventy senators that died
　By their proscriptions. Cicero being one.
Cassius: Cicero one?
Messala: 　　　　　　Cicero is dead,
　And by that order of proscription.
　Had you your letters from your wife, my lord?　　180
Brutus: No, Messala.
Messala: Nor nothing in your letters writ of her?
Brutus: Nothing, Messala.
Messala: 　　　　　　　　That, methinks, is strange.
Brutus: Why ask you? hear you aught of her in yours?
Messala: No, my lord.　　185
Brutus: Now, as you are a Roman, tell me true.
Messala: Then like a Roman bear the truth I tell:
　For certain she is dead, and by strange manner.
Brutus: Why, farewell Portia. We must die, Messala:
　With meditating that she must die once　　190
　I have the patience to endure it now.
Messala: Even so great men great losses should endure.
Cassius: I have as much of this in art as you,
　But yet my nature could not bear it so.
Brutus: Well, to our work alive. What do you think　　195
　Of marching to Philippi presently?

200   *Doing himself offence:* harming his chances

202   *of force:* of necessity or by strength of reason or logic

205   *grudged us contribution:* have been reluctant to supply us
206   *by them:* through their land

213   *tried ... friends:* have been given all the help our allies can
       give us

227   *we will niggard ... rest:* We will give in to nature's demand
       for sleep, but with as little as possible. "Niggard" is an old
       Norse word meaning stingy or scanty.

Cassius: I do not think it good.
Brutus: Your reason?
Cassius: This it is:
   'Tis better that the enemy seek us:
   So shall he waste his means, weary his soldiers,
   Doing himself offence; whilst we, lying still,   200
   Are full of rest, defence, and nimbleness.
Brutus: Good reasons must of force give place to better.
   The people 'twixt Philippi and this ground
   Do stand but in a forced affection,
   For they have grudged us contribution: 205
   The enemy, marching along by them,
   By them shall make a fuller number up,
   Come on refresh'd, new added, and encouraged;
   From which advantage shall we cut him off,
   If at Philippi we do face him there,   210
   These people at our back.
Cassius: Hear me, good brother.
Brutus: Under your pardon. You must note beside,
   That we have tried the utmost of our friends,
   Our legions are brim-full, our cause is ripe:
   The enemy increaseth every day;   215
   We, at the height, are ready to decline.
   There is a tide in the affairs of men
   Which taken at the flood leads on to fortune;
   Omitted, all the voyage of their life
   Is bound in shallows and in miseries.   220
   On such a full sea are we now afloat,
   And we must take the current when it serves,
   Or lose our ventures.
Cassius: Then, with your will, go on;
   We'll along ourselves, and meet them at Philippi.
Brutus: The deep of night is crept upon our talk,   225
   And nature must obey necessity;
   Which we will niggard with a little rest.
   There is no more to say?
Cassius: No more. Good night:
   Early to-morrow will we rise and hence.
Brutus: Lucius! [*Enter Lucius.*]   My gown. [*Exit Lucius.*] 230
   Farewell, good Messala:

239   *instrument:* probably a lute, lyre, or other stringed
        instrument, often used to accompany singing or recitation

241   *o'erwatch'd:* tired out by watching and waiting

249   *watch your pleasure:* be on guard for your orders

251   *It may be ... bethink me:* I may change my mind.

258   *an't:* if it

Good night, Titinius: noble, noble Cassius,
Good night, and good repose.
Cassius: O my dear brother!
  This was an ill beginning of the night:
  Never come such division 'tween our souls!   235
  Let it not, Brutus.
Brutus: Everything is well.
Cassius: Good night, my lord.
Brutus: Good night, good brother.
Titinius, Messala: Good night, Lord Brutus.
Brutus: Farewell, every one.
                          [Exeunt all but Brutus.]

  [Re-enter Lucius, with the gown.]

  Give me the gown. Where is thy instrument?
Lucius: Here in the tent.
Brutus: What, thou speak'st drowsily?   240
  Poor knave, I blame thee not; thou art o'erwatch'd.
  Call Claudius and some other of my men;
  I'll have them sleep on cushions in my tent.
Lucius: Varro and Claudius!

  [Enter Varro and Claudius.]

Varro: Calls my lord?   245
Brutus: I pray you, sirs, lie in my tent and sleep;
  It may be I shall raise you by-and-by
  On business to my brother Cassius.
Varro: So please you, we will stand and watch your pleasure.
Brutus: I will not have it so: lie down, good sirs;   250
  It may be I shall otherwise bethink me.
  Look, Lucius, here's the book I sought for so;
  I put it in the pocket of my gown.
                    [Varro and Claudius lie down.]
Lucius: I was sure your lordship did not give it me.
Brutus: Bear with me, good boy, I am much forgetful.   255
  Canst thou hold up thy heavy eyes awhile,
  And touch thy instrument a strain or two?
Lucius: Ay, my lord, an't please you.
Brutus: It does, my boy:
  I trouble thee too much, but thou art willing.

268   *leaden:* heavy; *mace:* a ceremonial rod or stick used as a symbol of authority when arresting a person. Death was believed to touch a doomed person on the shoulder with a mace.

273   *leaf:* page

280   *to stare:* to stand on end

290   *false:* out of tune

Lucius: It is my duty, sir. 260
Brutus: I should not urge thy duty past thy might;
   I know young bloods look for a time of rest.
Lucius: I have slept, my lord, already.
Brutus: It was well done; and thou shalt sleep again;
   I will not hold thee long: if I do live, 265
   I will be good to thee.   [*Music and a song.*]
   This is a sleepy tune. O murderous slumber,
   Lay'st thou thy leaden mace upon my boy,
   That plays thee music? Gentle knave, good night;
   I will not do thee so much wrong to wake thee: 270
   If thou dost nod, thou break'st thy instrument;
   I'll take it from thee; and, good boy, good night.
   Let me see, let me see; is not the leaf turn'd down
   Where I left reading? Here it is, I think.

[*Enter the Ghost of Cæsar.*]

   How ill this taper burns! Ha! who comes here? 275
   I think it is the weakness of mine eyes
   That shapes this monstrous apparition.
   It comes upon me. Art thou anything?
   Art thou some god, some angel, or some devil,
   That makest my blood cold and my hair to stare? 280
   Speak to me what thou art.
Ghost: Thy evil spirit, Brutus.
Brutus: Why comest thou?
Ghost: To tell thee thou shalt see me at Philippi.
Brutus: Well; then I shall see thee again?
Ghost: Ay, at Philippi. 285
Brutus: Why, I will see thee at Philippi, then.
                            [*Exit Ghost.*]
   Now I have taken heart thou vanishest:
   Ill spirit, I would hold more talk with thee.
   Boy, Lucius! Varro! Claudius! Sirs, awake! Claudius!
Lucius: The strings, my lord, are false. 290
Brutus: He thinks he still is at his instrument.
   Lucius, awake!
Lucius: My lord?
Brutus: Didst thou dream, Lucius, that thou so criedst out?
Lucius: My lord, I do not know that I did cry. 295

305   *commend me:* take my greetings to
306   *set ... before:* advance his forces early in the morning

Brutus: Yes, that thou didst: didst thou see any thing?
Lucius: Nothing, my lord.
Brutus: Sleep again, Lucius. Sirrah Claudius!
　　[*To Varro.*] Fellow thou, awake!
Varro: My lord?　　　　　　　　　　　　　　　　300
Claudius: My lord?
Brutus: Why did you so cry out, sirs, in your sleep?
Varro, Claudius: Did we, my lord?
Brutus:　　　　　　　　　　Ay: saw you anything?
Varro: No, my lord, I saw nothing.
Claudius:　　　　　　　　　　Nor I, my lord.
Brutus: Go and commend me to my brother Cassius;　　305
　　Bid him set on his powers betimes before,
　　And we will follow.
Varro, Claudius: It shall be done, my lord.　　　　[*Exeunt.*]

Act 4, Scene 3: Activities

1. Relationships under strain frequently fracture and bring out aspects of character not previously evident. Brutus and Cassius appear to have been friends for a long time, but now they argue. In your groups, discuss what you think has caused this rift in their relationship. What do you learn about each of them that you did not know before? Do you think the conflict between the two of them is satisfactorily resolved? In your journal, record what advice you might, as an adviser, offer the two of them about the dangers of disagreements at this crucial time in their campaign. You will have to include Scene 3 in order to complete this activity.

2. How do you feel about Cassius and Brutus after this quarrel scene? Has your opinion of either one or both of them changed? Discuss your ideas. Add to or adjust your profiles of these characters, if necessary, as a result of your discussion.

3. Imagine that you are an officer in Brutus's or Cassius's army, and you have been asked to give your opinion in answer to Brutus's question, "What do you think of marching to Philippi presently?" (Philippi was a city in Macedonia noted for its gold mines.) How do you respond? Record your answer in the diary you keep about military matters.

4. Some people believe that ghosts exist while others believe ghosts are simply the products of an overactive imagination. We have invented a category for this phenomenon called "the paranormal." In your journal, record your thoughts on this issue.

   Whether ghosts are real or not, Brutus seems tormented by visions that terrify him. As a director, how would you stage the "ghost" sequence? Write your stage directions so that the actor involved would know how to deal with the dialogue.

5. Two people talking to each other does not normally make for gripping drama. As a director of this play, how do you keep your audience focused enough on what Brutus and Cassius are talking about so they understand the major concepts and ramifications involved in the conversation? You might wish to discuss this with the members of your group before you write your instructions to the cast of your production. Present your final edited version of the conversation to the class for their responses.

Suppose, as a film director, that you were going to use this conversation as the beginning of your film. How might the rest of the play evolve from this conversation? Sketch it out and ask class members for their input.

6. Melodrama is a theatrical convention in which the author plays upon the emotions of the audience in order to create sympathy for the characters. In your journal, decide whether or not you think Shakespeare uses this technique in this scene.

In early twentieth century movies, melodramatic scenes were always accompanied by music to reinforce the mood. Create or select some music to accompany the parts of this scene (or the one before it) that you consider to be melodramatic. Present your adaptation to the class.

7. In a brief essay, present your arguments for combining Scenes 2 and 3.

Act 4: Consider the Whole Act

1. You are employed by a major news network and your assignment is to create a news report on the events that have occurred since the assassination of Caesar. Film a series of interviews that you do with the public to capture their perspectives on the current events. The interviews can also be tape-recorded or even entirely written.

   Remember your audience and be sure to ask questions that elicit answers that viewers want to hear. You might want to ask the people you interview what they think might be the outcome of the ensuing battle at Philippi, and what might happen if Antony loses or if Brutus does. Create a poll in your class, tally the results, and present your findings.

2. Antony, Octavius, and Lepidus are carrying out what amounts to a reign of terror in Rome. Research other times and places in history where this kind of thing occurred in order to change the existing political system. What aspects do these circumstances share? Are the results similar? Are there any patterns to these events? You might want to note which of them succeeded and which of them failed.

   Select one of these political events and use it as a basis to suggest what must have been going on in Rome in 44 B.C.E. and what the outcome might have been. Historically, what was the outcome?

   Prepare a written account of your findings and conclusions for presentation as a news article to be published for the class to read.

3. You are a foreign correspondent assigned to cover the events at Philippi. You have been granted a brief interview with Brutus just before he leaves for the battle. You meet him outside his tent and ask five key questions. What are they? Remember, the purpose of your questions is to get as much information as you can about Brutus's strategic

plans, his objectives, and perhaps even his doubts and fears. Since there were no video cameras available in 44 B.C.E., you will have to create a drawing that best illustrates the scene.

4. *Make a video*

Choose a conversation between two important characters in this act. Rehearse your reading of the chosen lines with a partner to clarify the meaning you want to convey to your audience. Consider things such as stance, body movement, gestures, facial expressions, and personal interactions with the other character.

As you prepare a shooting script, keep in mind the following:

- Consider the distance between the camera and your subject. Changing the distance will change the size of the subject and the balance of the shot. These changes will alter the mood.
- Determine the kind of lighting to best convey the mood you want to create.
- Decide on the angles you think will be most effective.
- Provide one visual shot per complete thought.
- Design an audio lead-in of appropriate music before the visual portion actually begins. The scene could be ended in the same manner.

For the next scene ...

Imagine you and a partner are about to enter an important competition against strong opponents. What would you say to your partner just before the match?

Act 5, Scene 1

In this scene ...

The action now moves to the plains of Philippi where the armies of Octavius and Antony are camped. A messenger announces the arrival of their enemies, the armies of Brutus and Cassius. Octavius decides to lead his forces from the right of the field, thereby overruling Antony's directions.

Brutus and Cassius enter with their armies and engage in a verbal battle with Octavius and Antony. Octavius challenges Brutus to more active combat and withdraws his forces. While Brutus and his officer move aside to talk, Cassius confides to Messala his doubts about the threatening circumstances in which he finds himself.

Alone on stage, Brutus and Cassius consider the possible outcomes of this day. They exchange farewells and part to face the victory or defeat that lies ahead.

4	*battles:* armies
5	*warn:* challenge
7	*in their bosoms:* in on their secrets
10	*face:* appearance
11	*To fasten in our thoughts:* to persuade us

14   *bloody sign:* a red flag indicating that the fighting is about to begin, from which we get our expression "waving a red flag."

16   *softly on:* slowly but steadily forward

17   *Upon the left hand:* The left was considered to be the "weak" side; taking the right side would have suggested superiority. We still have some of this bias today. *even:* level

19   *exigent:* crisis

21   *They ... parley:* They are stopping and asking for a conference.

Act 5, Scene 1

The Plains of Philippi.
Enter Octavius, Antony, and their
army.

Octavius: Now, Antony, our hopes are answered:
    You said the enemy would not come down,
    But keep the hills and upper regions;
    It proves not so: their battles are at hand;
    They mean to warn us at Philippi here,   5
    Answering before we do demand of them.
Antony: Tut, I am in their bosoms, and I know
    Wherefore they do it: they could be content
    To visit other places; and come down
    With fearful bravery, thinking by this face   10
    To fasten in our thoughts that they have courage;
    But 'tis not so.

[*Enter a Messenger.*]

Messenger: Prepare you, generals:
    The enemy comes on in gallant show;
    Their bloody sign of battle is hung out,
    And something to be done immediately.   15
Antony: Octavius, lead your battle softly on,
    Upon the left hand of the even field.
Octavius: Upon the right hand I; keep thou the left.
Antony: Why do you cross me in this exigent?
Octavius: I do not cross you; but I will do so.   [*March.*]   20

[*Drum. Enter Brutus, Cassius, and their army; Lucilius,*
    Titinius, Messala, and others.]

Brutus: They stand, and would have parley.
Cassius: Stand fast, Titinius: we must out and talk.
Octavius: Mark Antony, shall we give sign of battle?

24	*answer on their charge:* meet them when they attack
25	*Make forth:* go forward

33	*The posture of your blows:* your skill as a soldier
34	*Hybla:* a mountain town in Sicily well known for its sweet honey

41	*show'd your teeth:* grinned or grimaced
43	*cur:* a mongrel dog, a cowardly person
45–47	*Now, Brutus, ... ruled:* Cassius reminds Brutus that if Cassius had had his way and convinced him to kill Antony as well, this confrontation would not have happened.
48	*Come ... cause:* Get to the point.
49	*proof of it:* test to decide the argument

52	*goes up again:* is returned to its sheath

55	*Have added slaughter to:* has also been killed by. Octavius may be speaking of himself.

59	*strain:* family or lineage

Antony: No, Cæsar, we will answer on their charge.
  Make forth; the generals would have some words. 25
Octavius: Stir not until the signal.
Brutus: Words before blows: is it so, countrymen?
Octavius: Not that we love words better, as you do.
Brutus: Good words are better than bad strokes, Octavius.
Antony: In your bad strokes, Brutus, you give good words: 30
  Witness the hole you made in Cæsar's heart,
  Crying "Long live! hail, Cæsar!"
Cassius: Antony,
  The posture of your blows are yet unknown:
  But for your words, they rob the Hybla bees,
  And leave them honeyless.
Antony: Not stingless too. 35
Brutus: O, yes, and soundless too;
  For you have stol'n their buzzing, Antony,
  And very wisely threat before you sting.
Antony: Villains, you did not so, when your vile daggers
  Hack'd one another in the sides of Cæsar: 40
  You show'd your teeth like apes, and fawn'd like hounds,
  And bow'd like bondmen, kissing Cæsar's feet;
  Whilst damned Casca, like a cur, behind
  Struck Cæsar on the neck. O you flatterers!
Cassius: Flatterers! Now, Brutus, thank yourself: 45
  This tongue had not offended so to-day,
  If Cassius might have ruled.
Octavius: Come, come, the cause: if arguing make us sweat;
  The proof of it will turn to redder drops.
  Look; 50
  I draw a sword against conspirators;
  When think you that the sword goes up again?
  Never, till Cæsar's three and thirty wounds
  Be well avenged, or till another Cæsar
  Have added slaughter to the sword of traitors. 55
Brutus: Cæsar, thou canst not die by traitors' hands,
  Unless thou bring'st them with thee.
Octavius: So I hope;
  I was not born to die on Brutus' sword.
Brutus: O, if thou wert the noblest of thy strain,
  Young man, thou couldst not die more honourable. 60

61   *peevish:* childish, pouting. Octavius was only 21 at the time, and apparently Antony had a reputation as a "reveller."

66   *when you have stomachs:* when you have the courage

68   *on the hazard:* at stake

77   *I held Epicurus strong:* Epicureanism taught that because the gods were not interested in anything humans did, any phenomenon resembling an omen was meaningless and should be ignored. However, when Cassius senses the end is near, he decides that Epicurus must have been incorrect; the birds that are behaving strangely convince him that something ominous is about to happen.

79   *presage:* foretell events

80   *former:* first, foremost

81   *Two mighty eagles fell:* The eagle was both the symbol of the might of the Roman armies and of good fortune. These eagles are seen behaving strangely. *fell:* swooped down

83   *consorted:* accompanied

85   *ravens, crows and kites:* scavengers, as well as symbols of death. These birds followed armies, knowing corpses would eventually result.

87   *sickly:* literally "sick" and on the verge of death

88   *fatal:* fated, predicting death

91   *resolved:* determined

92   *constantly:* without wavering (in my beliefs)

Cassius: A peevish schoolboy, worthless of such honour,
    Join'd with a masker and a reveller!
Antony: Old Cassius still!
Octavius: Come, Antony, away!
    Defiance, traitors, hurl we in your teeth:
    If you dare fight to-day, come to the field;   65
    If not, when you have stomachs.
                    [Exeunt Octavius, Antony, and their army.]
Cassius: Why, now, blow wind, swell billow and swim bark!
    The storm is up, and all is on the hazard.
Brutus: Ho, Lucilius! hark, a word with you.
Lucilius [Standing forth]:   My lord?
                [Brutus and Lucilius converse apart.]
Cassius: Messala!   70
Messala [Standing forth]: What says my general?
Cassius: Messala,
    This is my birthday; as this very day
    Was Cassius born. Give me thy hand, Messala:
    Be thou my witness that against my will,
    As Pompey was, am I compell'd to set   75
    Upon one battle all our liberties.
    You know that I held Epicurus strong
    And his opinion: now I change my mind,
    And partly credit things that do presage.
    Coming from Sardis, on our former ensign   80
    Two mighty eagles fell, and there they perch'd
    Gorging and feeding from our soldiers' hands;
    Who to Philippi here consorted us:
    This morning are they fled away and gone;
    And in their steads do ravens, crows and kites   85
    Fly o'er our heads and downward look on us,
    As we were sickly prey: their shadows seem
    A canopy most fatal, under which
    Our army lies, ready to give up the ghost.
Messala: Believe not so.
Cassius: I but believe it partly: 90
    For I am fresh of spirit and resolved
    To meet all perils very constantly.
Brutus: Even so, Lucilius.
Cassius: Now, most noble Brutus,

101   *that philosophy:* Stoicism—a reference to the Stoic belief that pain and suffering were natural to life and should be endured willingly

102–103   *Cato:* a bitter opponent of Caesar who fought with Pompey. After the followers of Pompey were defeated, Cato committed suicide rather than be captured by Caesar. Stoicism, which appears to have been Brutus's philosophy, denounces suicide, but he decides that death is preferable to capture and dishonour.

107   *providence:* divine will

The gods to-day stand friendly, that we may,
Lovers in peace, lead on our days to age!   95
But since the affairs of men rest still incertain,
Let's reason with the worst that may befall.
If we do lose this battle, then is this
The very last time we shall speak together:
What are you then determined to do?   100
Brutus: Even by the rule of that philosophy
By which I did blame Cato for the death
Which he did give himself; I know not how,
But I do find it cowardly and vile,
For fear of what might fall, so to prevent   105
The time of life: arming myself with patience
To stay the providence of some high powers
That govern us below.
Cassius: Then, if we lose this battle,
You are contented to be led in triumph
Thorough the streets of Rome?   110
Brutus: No, Cassius, no: think not, thou noble Roman,
That ever Brutus will go bound to Rome:
He bears too great a mind. But this same day
Must end that work the Ides of March begun;
And whether we shall meet again I know not.   115
Therefore our everlasting farewell take:
For ever and for ever, farewell, Cassius!
If we do meet again, why, we shall smile;
If not, why then this parting was well made.
Cassius: For ever and for ever, farewell, Brutus!   120
If we do meet again, we'll smile indeed;
If not, 'tis true this parting was well made.
Brutus: Why, then, lead on. O, that a man might know
The end of this day's business ere it come!
But it sufficeth that the day will end,   125
And then the end is known. Come, ho! away!
                                                        [*Exeunt.*]

Act 5, Scene 1: Activities

1. This scene gives us more information concerning Octavius's character. How would you describe his words and actions? Has Octavius or your opinion of him changed from his earlier appearance in the play? If you created an earlier biography or profile of him, update it now. If not, write a short entry for Octavius to be published in the *Who's Who in Rome* for 42 B.C.E.

2. Flashbacks are used in films and television productions to show what happened earlier in the story. As a director filming this scene, you choose to include flashbacks during the argument that occurs between the two sets of enemies.

    a) In your group, decide on two events or exchanges from earlier in the play that you would use as flashbacks. Decide who would be experiencing each flashback, and at what points during the argument you would insert them.

    b) Compare your flashbacks and the places you inserted them with the ones other groups have selected.

3. In your journal, record your feelings toward Cassius as he bids farewell to Brutus at the end of this scene. If you have been developing a profile of Cassius, notice how this entry compares with ones you made earlier. How is it the same? different? Share your observations with others.

4. Portents and omens play a major role in the play, though what they actually mean is never quite clear. With your group, make a list of the major omens in the play, explain each as best you can, and decide how the characters' interpretations of them really do affect the outcome of the play.

5. In a movie or a story, the ending is usually the logical outcome of situations and events that occured earlier. In this scene, there are several clues about future events.

Select lines from this scene that provide these clues. With a partner, discuss your choices and explain why you think Shakespeare provides the audience with this guiding information.

6. One of the rules of battle was that the opposing leaders should talk to each other on the battlefield before the actual conflict began. This meeting usually consisted of insults, accusations, and other behaviour that we might consider to be pointless. However, the meeting did give each of the commanders the chance to assess the other. How does this work in this scene? Who seems to you to be more in control? Who seems most eager to fight?

As a war photographer, you must record this meeting. Decide how you are going to arrange this photo by sketching your composition, making sure that you include the armies in the background of your photograph or drawing. Include your impressions of what you saw and heard on the day you took this picture.

For the next scenes ...

Recall a situation you experienced or know about in which one or more people totally misinterpreted the evidence in front of them. What happened?

Act 5, Scenes 2 and 3

In these scenes ...

Brutus crosses the battlefield, giving orders for his wing to attack the soldiers of Octavius.

A tired and defeated Cassius arrives in another part of the field. He believes that all is lost. With the help of his servant Pindarus, he commits suicide, dying upon the same sword with which he stabbed Caesar.

Titinius, who was sent by Cassius to appraise the field, returns with the news that Brutus has defeated Octavius. He has arrived too late, however. He discovers the dead Cassius and, in the Roman tradition of showing respect and loyalty toward his leader, Titinius kills himself. Brutus enters and, grieving, pays tribute to Cassius and Titinius. He then orders his armies to a second battle.

1   *bills:* written orders
2   *the other side:* not the enemy, but another wing of their own army, one led by Cassius
4   *but cold demeanour:* no enthusiastic desire to fight
5   *push:* attack

Scene 2

The same. The field of battle.
Alarum. Enter Brutus and Messala.

Brutus: Ride, ride, Messala, ride and give these bills
    Unto the legions on the other side.   [*Loud alarum.*]
    Let them set on at once; for I perceive
    But cold demeanour in Octavius' wing,
    And sudden push gives them the overthrow.   5
    Ride, ride, Messala; let them all come down.
                       [*Exeunt.*]

1   *villains:* Cassius is referring to his own troops.
2   *mine own:* my own soldiers
3   *ensign:* flag-bearer

7   *fell to spoil:* began looting

19   *even with a thought:* as quickly as a thought travels

21   *thick:* weak, nearsighted

25   *run his compass:* completed its circle from beginning to end

Scene 3

Another part of the field.
Alarums. Enter Cassius and
Titinius.

Cassius: O, look, Titinius, look, the villains fly!
  Myself have to mine own turn'd enemy:
  This ensign here of mine was turning back;
  I slew the coward, and did take it from him.
Titinius: O Cassius, Brutus gave the word too early: 5
  Who, having some advantage on Octavius,
  Took it too eagerly: his soldiers fell to spoil,
  Whilst we by Antony are all enclosed.

[*Enter Pindarus.*]

Pindarus: Fly further off, my lord, fly further off;
  Mark Antony is in your tents, my lord: 10
  Fly, therefore, noble Cassius, fly far off.
Cassius: This hill is far enough. Look, look, Titinius;
  Are those my tents where I perceive the fire?
Titinius: They are, my lord.
Cassius: Titinius, if thou lovest me,
  Mount thou my horse and hide thy spurs in him,   15
  Till he have brought thee up to yonder troops
  And here again; that I may rest assured
  Whether yond troops are friend or enemy.
Titinius: I will be here again, even with a thought.
                                     [*Exit.*]
Cassius: Go, Pindarus, get higher on that hill;   20
  My sight was ever thick; regard Titinius,
  And tell me what thou notest about the field.
                        [*Pindarus ascends the hill.*]
  This day I breathed first: time is come round,
  And where I did begin, there shall I end;
  My life is run his compass. Sirrah, what news?   25
Pindarus [*Above*]: O my lord!

28   *Above:* This stage direction likely refers to the upper stage in an Elizabethan theatre, as well as to the top of the hill in the battlefield.

31   *lights:* dismounts (from his horse)

32   *ta'en:* taken, captured

38   *swore thee:* made you swear

42   *search:* run through; *bosom:* breast, chest

43   *Stand not:* do not hesitate; *hilts:* handle of the sword

48   *Durst ... will:* if I had dared to do as I wished

51   *change:* The situation has changed for the better. Fortune was generally considered to be unpredictable.

Cassius: What news?
Pindarus [*Above*]: Titinius is enclosed round about
    With horsemen, that make to him on the spur;
    Yet he spurs on. Now they are almost on him.   30
    Now, Titinius! Now some light. O, he lights too.
    He's ta'en. [*Shout.*] And, hark! they shout for joy.
Cassius: Come down, behold no more.
    O coward that I am, to live so long,
    To see my best friend ta'en before my face!   35
                         [*Pindarus descends.*]
    Come hither, sirrah:
    In Parthia did I take thee prisoner;
    And then I swore thee, saving of thy life,
    That whatsoever I did bid thee do,
    Thou shouldst attempt it. Come now, keep thine oath;   40
    Now be a freeman: and with this good sword,
    That ran through Cæsar's bowels, search this bosom.
    Stand not to answer: here, take thou the hilts;
    And when my face is cover'd, as 'tis now,
    Guide thou the sword. [*Pindarus stabs him.*] Cæsar, thou
      art revenged,   45
    Even with the sword that kill'd thee.   [*Dies.*]
Pindarus: So, I am free; yet would not so have been,
    Durst I have done my will. O Cassius!
    Far from this country Pindarus shall run,
    Where never Roman shall take note of him.   [*Exit.*]   50

[*Re-enter Titinius with Messala.*]

Messala: It is but change, Titinius; for Octavius
    Is overthrown by noble Brutus' power,
    As Cassius' legions are by Antony.
Titinius: These tidings will well comfort Cassius.
Messala: Where did you leave him?
Titinius: All disconsolate,   55
    With Pindarus his bondman, on this hill.
Messala: Is not that he that lies upon the ground?
Titinius: He lies not like the living. O my heart!
Messala: Is not that he?
Titinius: No, this was he, Messala,
    But Cassius is no more. O setting sun,   60

67   *O ... child:* What terrible mistakes and misunderstandings are caused by people who suffer from and act on their depression and desperation, and their fear of imaginary threats.

68   *apt thoughts:* easily impressed or influenced

71   *the mother:* the melancholic Cassius who caused the fatal error

84   *misconstrued:* misunderstood

87   *apace:* quickly

89   *Roman's part:* It was considered an honourable act to show one's loyalty to a friend or superior officer by dying with him for the same cause.

As in thy red rays thou dost sink to night,
So in his red blood Cassius' day is set;
The sun of Rome is set. Our day is gone;
Clouds, dews, and dangers come; our deeds are done!
Mistrust of my success hath done this deed.   65
Messala: Mistrust of good success hath done this deed.
O hateful error, melancholy's child,
Why dost thou show to the apt thoughts of men
The things that are not? O error, soon conceived,
Thou never comest unto a happy birth,   70
But kill'st the mother that engender'd thee!
Titinius: What, Pindarus! where art thou, Pindarus?
Messala: Seek him, Titinius, whilst I go to meet
The noble Brutus, thrusting this report
Into his ears: I may say, thrusting it;   75
For piercing steel and darts envenomed
Shall be as welcome to the ears of Brutus
As tidings of this sight.
Titinius: Hie you, Messala,
And I will seek for Pindarus the while.
                              [*Exit Messala.*]
Why didst thou send me forth, brave Cassius?   80
Did I not meet thy friends? and did not they
Put on my brows this wreath of victory,
And bid me give it thee? Didst thou not hear their shouts?
Alas, thou hast misconstrued every thing!
But, hold thee, take this garland on thy brow;   85
Thy Brutus bid me give it thee, and I
Will do his bidding. Brutus, come apace,
And see how I regarded Caius Cassius.
By your leave, gods: this is a Roman's part:
Come Cassius' sword, and find Titinius' heart.
                              [*Kills himself.*]   90

[*Alarum. Re-enter Messala, with Brutus, young Cato, and
    Lucilius and others.*]

Brutus: Where, where, Messala, doth his body lie?
Messala: Lo, yonder, and Titinius mourning it.
Brutus: Titinius' face is upward.
Cato: He is slain.

101   *fellow:* equal

104   *Thasos:* an island in the Aegean Sea near Philippi

106   *discomfort:* upset or dispirit the troops

Brutus: O Julius Cæsar, thou art mighty yet!
    Thy spirit walks abroad, and turns our swords   95
    In our own proper entrails.   [*Low alarums.*]
Cato: Brave Titinius!
    Look whether he have not crown'd dead Cassius!
Brutus: Are yet two Romans living such as these?
    The last of all the Romans, fare thee well!
    It is impossible that ever Rome   100
    Should breed thy fellow. Friends, I owe more tears
    To this dead man than you shall see me pay.
    I shall find time, Cassius, I shall find time.
    Come therefore, and to Thasos send his body:
    His funerals shall not be in our camp,   105
    Lest it discomfort us. Lucilius, come;
    And come, young Cato; let us to the field.
    Labeo and Flavius, set our battles on.
    'Tis three o'clock; and, Romans, yet ere night
    We shall try fortune in a second fight.   [*Exeunt.*]   110

Act 5, Scenes 2 and 3: Activities

1. Write a testimonial (a long obituary) for Cassius as it might appear today in a national newspaper or news magazine.

2. If you had been with Cassius just before he took his life, what might you have said to him to attempt to prevent him from committing suicide? Summarize what is said earlier in the play that seems to contradict his decision to have Pindarus kill him at this point.

3. Cassius followed the philosophy of Epicureanism. With the assistance of your teacher and/or librarian, find out how followers of Epicureanism viewed suicide. How would you adjust your comments to Cassius from activity 2 to allow for his beliefs? What would you add or say differently?

4. Most movies that include battle scenes are shot on location or on large sets. On stage, however, it is very difficult to create the illusion of large and chaotic battles. How does Shakespeare keep his audience aware of the battle that is taking place throughout most of the act? How does he create a sense of both the physical and the emotional aspects of battle?

   With your group, create a stage diagram that indicates how you, as director, would give the impression of large-scale and intense fighting. As an alternative, you could create a collage or a map to show the same thing.

5. If you were one of Brutus's officers or advisers in this scene, what advice would you give him about his military position at present? What plan of attack would you recommend he follow for his "second fight"? You may wish to do some research on battles of ancient Roman times before answering this question.

   Present the results of your research and your military counsel to Brutus in an oral report to classmates. You could include diagrams, maps, and charts to illustrate your military planning.

6. Create a logistical or relief map that depicts and clarifies what occurred historically at the battle of Philippi. With the help of your teacher and/or librarian, research the events of the battle and translate them into a clear visual format. Your map could be in any of a two-dimensional, three-dimensional, or virtual form. You might check current news magazines or evening news broadcasts for examples of this type of map. Your final version could be included as part of a Web site you construct on Caesar's Assassination and its Consequences.

For the next scenes ...

What qualities in a person's character can help him or her to continue in a competitive struggle even when winning seems unlikely?

Act 5, Scenes 4 and 5

In these scenes ...

The battle continues as Brutus, young Cato, and Lucilius are engaged in hand-to-hand combat with their enemy. Soon, Lucilius, one of Brutus's most important officers, is captured. It is apparent that Octavius and Antony are emerging as the winners.

Brutus appears with the remnants of his weary army. In spite of his officers' attempts to encourage him, Brutus is convinced that all is lost, that his enemies have won. At the sound of the enemies' approach, he bids his soldiers farewell and orders them to flee to a safer spot. He and his servant Strato stay. He gives Strato his sword and orders him to hold it forward. Brutus ends his life by running upon the sword.

The victors arrive. Seeing the fallen Brutus before him, Antony praises Brutus as "the noblest Roman of them all," and Octavius, Caesar's successor, delivers a final tribute. He proclaims the battle ended, promises a soldier's funeral with all honours for Brutus, and departs from the field to share in the glories of his victory.

2   *bastard:* person of low or inferior origins

4   *Marcus Cato:* brother of Portia, Brutus's wife

7–8   Lines 7 and 8 in this scene are sometimes given to Lucilius
         because Plutarch indicates that Lucilius is impersonating
         Brutus here. However, the Folio does not make it at all clear
         that this is intended.

12   *Only ... die:* I will surrender only if you will kill me.
13   *straight:* immediately

14   *Kill Brutus ... in his death:* Lucilius is impersonating Brutus
         in order to mislead the enemy and protect his leader.

Scene 4

Another part of the field.
Alarum. Enter fighting, Soldiers of
both armies; among them Brutus,
young Cato, and Lucilius.

Brutus: Yet, countrymen, O yet hold up your heads!
Cato: What bastard doth not? Who will go with me?
  I will proclaim my name about the field.
  I am the son of Marcus Cato, ho!
  A foe to tyrants, and my country's friend;   5
  I am the son of Marcus Cato, ho!
Brutus: And I am Brutus, Marcus Brutus, I;
  Brutus, my country's friend; know me for Brutus!
                         [Exit. Cato falls.]
Lucilius: O young and noble Cato, art thou down?
  Why, now thou diest as bravely as Titinius;   10
  And mayst be honour'd, being Cato's son.
First Soldier: Yield, or thou diest.
Lucilius: Only I yield to die;
  There is so much that thou wilt kill me straight;
                       [Offering money.]
  Kill Brutus, and be honour'd in his death.
First Soldier: We must not. A noble prisoner!   15
Second Soldier: Room, ho! Tell Antony, Brutus is ta'en.
First Soldier: I'll tell the news. Here comes the general.

  [Enter Antony.]

  Brutus is ta'en, Brutus is ta'en, my lord.
Antony: Where is he?
Lucilius: Safe, Antony; Brutus is safe enough: 20
  I dare assure thee that no enemy
  Shall ever take alive the noble Brutus:

25   *like himself:* behaving as the noble Roman he was

32   *is chanced:* has turned out

The gods defend him from so great a shame!
When you do find him, or alive or dead,
He will be found like Brutus, like himself.   25
Antony: This is not Brutus, friend; but, I assure you,
A prize no less in worth: keep this man safe;
Give him all kindness: I had rather have
Such men my friends than enemies. Go on,
And see whether Brutus be alive or dead;   30
And bring us word unto Octavius' tent
How everything is chanced.   [*Exeunt.*]

2   *show'd the torch-light:* (Statilius) went to Cassius's camp to see if it had been captured by the enemy and held up his torch to indicate that all was well there. However, he was obviously captured shortly after.

13   *vessel:* a container; a metaphor for a human being

15   *list:* listen or hear

18   *several:* separate

23   *pit:* a trap for capturing wild animals, as well as a grave

Scene 5

Another part of the field.
Enter Brutus, Dardanius, Clitus,
Strato, and Volumnius.

Brutus: Come, poor remains of friends, rest on this rock.
Clitus: Statilius show'd the torch-light, but, my lord,
   He came not back: he is or ta'en or slain.
Brutus: Sit thee down, Clitus: slaying is the word;
   It is a deed in fashion. Hark thee, Clitus.   5
                   [*Whispering.*]
Clitus: What, I, my lord? No, not for all the world.
Brutus: Peace then, no words.
Clitus: I'll rather kill myself.
Brutus: Hark thee, Dardanius.   [*Whispering.*]
Dardanius: Shall I do such a deed?
Clitus: O Dardanius!
Dardanius: O Clitus!   10
Clitus: What ill request did Brutus make to thee?
Dardanius: To kill him, Clitus. Look, he meditates.
Clitus: Now is that noble vessel full of grief,
   That it runs over even at his eyes.
Brutus: Come hither, good Volumnius; list a word.   15
Volumnius: What says my lord?
Brutus: Why this, Volumnius:
   The ghost of Cæsar hath appear'd to me
   Two several times by night; at Sardis once,
   And this last night here in Philippi fields:
   I know my hour is come.
Volumnius: Not so, my lord.   20
Brutus: Nay, I am sure it is, Volumnius.
   Thou seest the world, Volumnius, how it goes;
   Our enemies have beat us to the pit: [*Low alarums.*]
   It is more worthy to leap in ourselves,
   Than tarry till they push us. Good Volumnius,   25

29   *office:* job, task

46   *smatch:* touch, taste

53   *man:* servant, bondman

Thou know'st that we two went to school together:
Even for that our love of old, I prithee,
Hold thou my sword-hilts, whilst I run on it.
Volumnius: That's not an office for a friend, my lord.
[*Alarum still.*]

Clitus: Fly, fly, my lord; there is no tarrying here.   30
Brutus: Farewell to you; and you; and you, Volumnius.
  Strato, thou hast been all this while asleep;
  Farewell to thee too, Strato. Countrymen,
  My heart doth joy that yet in all my life
  I found no man but he was true to me.   35
  I shall have glory by this losing day,
  More than Octavius and Mark Antony
  By this vile conquest shall attain unto.
  So, fare you well at once; for Brutus' tongue
  Hath almost ended his life's history: 40
  Night hangs upon mine eyes; my bones would rest,
  That have but labour'd to attain this hour.
[*Alarum. Cry within:* "Fly, fly, fly!"]

Clitus: Fly, my lord, fly!
Brutus: Hence! I will follow.
[*Exeunt Clitus, Dardanius, and Volumnius.*]

  I prithee, Strato, stay thou by thy lord:
  Thou art a fellow of a good respect;   45
  Thy life hath had some smatch of honour in it:
  Hold then my sword, and turn away thy face,
  While I do run upon it. Wilt thou, Strato?
Strato: Give me your hand first. Fare you well, my lord.
Brutus: Farewell, good Strato. [*Runs on his sword.*] Cæsar,
  now be still: 50
  I kill'd not thee with half so good a will.   [*Dies.*]

[*Alarum. Retreat. Enter Octavius, Antony, Messala, Lucilius,
  and the Army.*]

Octavius: What man is that?
Messala: My master's man. Strato, where is thy master?
Strato: Free from the bondage you are in, Messala:
  The conquerors can but make a fire of him;   55
  For Brutus only overcame himself,
  And no man else hath honour by his death.

60   *entertain:* take into my service
61   *bestow thy time with me:* spend your life in my service
62   *prefer:* recommend

67   *latest:* last, final

72   *made:* became
73   *gentle:* noble; *elements:* the four elements believed to make up all nature: earth, air, fire, and water
74   *so mix'd in him:* so well balanced
76   *use:* treat

79   *Most ... honourably:* given full military honours
80   *field:* army
81   *part:* divide

Lucilius: So Brutus should be found. I thank thee, Brutus,
    That thou has proved Lucilius' saying true.
Octavius: All that served Brutus, I will entertain them.   60
    Fellow, wilt thou bestow thy time with me?
Strato: Ay, if Messala will prefer me to you.
Octavius: Do so, good Messala.
Messala: How died my master, Strato:
Strato: I held the sword, and he did run on it.   65
Messala: Octavius, then take him to follow thee,
    That did the latest service to my master.
Antony: This was the noblest Roman of them all:
    All the conspirators, save only he,
    Did that they did in envy of great Cæsar;   70
    He only, in a general honest thought
    And common good to all, made one of them.
    His life was gentle, and the elements
    So mix'd in him that Nature might stand up
    And say to all the world "This was a man!"   75
Octavius: According to his virtue let us use him,
    With all respect and rites of burial.
    Within my tent his bones to-night shall lie,
    Most like a soldier, order'd honourably.
    So call the field to rest; and let's away,   80
    To part the glories of this happy day.
                         [*Exeunt omnes.*]

Act 5, Scenes 4 and 5: Activities

1. Record a final entry about Brutus in your journal. What happens in these scenes to confirm and/or deepen your understanding of this man?

2. Look back in this act to the last words Cassius said to Pindarus before he died (Scene 3, lines 33–46) and the ones that Brutus said to his officers and servant (Scene 5, lines 31–42). Why is each speech effective as a final farewell?

   How are their speeches similar? In what ways does each speech confirm or add to your understanding of each of these leading characters? Which of the two men would you have preferred as a best friend? Why?

3. Write a speech that could be part of a funeral oration delivered by Antony at Brutus's funeral. Include some of the feelings that Antony expresses in his final speech of the play. Record your speech on tape or on paper and share it with others.

4. Earlier in Act 5, Titinius, despairing over Cassius's death, cries, "Alas, thou hast misconstrued every thing!" Discuss which other characters in the play have also misunderstood actions or words and what the consequences of each misunderstanding were. Use evidence from the text to support your views in an explanatory essay of at least 500 words.

5. With your group, write a newspaper article or prepare a news report for radio or television on the final events in the play.

   - Bring your audience up to date on the final outcome of the political and military conflict that has been occurring.
   - Include street interviews with some of the citizens of Rome and the soldiers who are returning from the wars.
   - Make some final predictions about Octavius's chances of restoring law and order to the Roman Empire.

Present your article or report to your class. Compare your account with those of other groups. Discuss similarities and differences in the various presentations.

6. Suppose Brutus does not die but is captured and brought before Octavius and Antony. With the help of a partner, create a scene in which Brutus's fate is determined. What will happen to him in your version? How will he act during this final confrontation? Could it be possible for Octavius and Antony to offer him a share of their power? Present your rewritten ending to the class.

Consider the Whole Play

1. Review the actions of both Brutus and Antony in this play. List the problems that Brutus faced on one side of the page, and note the actions he took to deal with them on the other side. Do the same with Antony. Could either one have changed the course of events by acting differently? Explain your answer. Share your responses with others in your group or class.

2. Write a political commentary of the play as it might appear in a newspaper or magazine you know. You might include topics such as the following:

   • social violence
   • loyalty and trust between friends
   • ambitious leaders and blind followers
   • defeat and victory
   • state control

3. Identify a social or political issue that is a concern in your community, country, or another part of the world. Select a character from the play *Julius Caesar* whose experiences might have included elements related to the issue. With a partner, interview the character. Ask questions that would require the character to explain how he or she would

handle the problem. Record the conversation and share it with an audience.

4. At the end of the play, Octavius begins his career as a political leader. From what you have observed about him, make some predictions about what you think he might have accomplished during his reign. After you have listed your ideas, investigate some reference materials on his life and his rule. Compare your findings with your predictions. Share your discoveries with others.

5. a) Review the illustrations that appear throughout this text. With your group, discuss your responses to some of these visuals, including your comments about the following:

   - what the scenes describe
   - what feelings you have as you consider the illustrations and what aspect(s) of each one prompt those feelings
   - what value the illustrations have for the text of a play
   - whether you agree with the choice of events depicted and, if not, what other choices you might have made

   b) Create your own illustration for one or more of the scenes. Before you begin, consider the following questions:

   - What moment or event from the scene will you depict?
   - What character(s) will you include and how much background detail is necessary?
   - What emotion do you want your viewer to feel as he or she studies your illustration? How will you convey that emotion?

6. Design a poster for an upcoming production of *Julius Caesar*. The job of a poster is to instantly attract the attention of potential audience members by using colours, shapes, and images to communicate an aspect of the play in an interesting way. In selecting your poster image(s), consider what central theme or idea from the play you feel would work best to attract people who may be unfamiliar

with the story. You might look at the cover illustration and other illustrations in this text for possible ideas, or research movies and other productions of the play. Do rough sketches of all your ideas and show them to your partner or group to check their effectiveness. Select one, make any changes you feel are necessary, then hang your finished posters in a class display.

7. There are many examples in history of military figures who became powerful political leaders. With the help of your librarian or teacher, select one of these military figures and prepare a written profile on the individual. Compare the personality and career of this person with that of Julius Caesar.

8. Imagine that a touring production of *Julius Caesar* is coming to your community. You want to encourage people to attend a performance. Prepare a slide show of events from the play to attract an audience. Use members of your class to stage the events appropriate to your purpose. Photograph each of these incidents on slides. Write a monologue to connect the incidents. Choose appropriate background music for your slides so that the whole presentation makes an emotional impact. Present your slide show to an audience.

9. You are a director. Select part of a scene that you particularly like and do the following:

   - Decide what you think its main idea is.
   - Discuss with the actors who will play the scene how they will speak the lines and how they will present the action.
   - Create a prompt book in which you make notes to yourself about such decisions as stage directions, pauses, points of emphasis, and lighting and sound cues.

   Direct the scene using this prompt book. After suitable rehearsal time, present the scene to the class. Follow the performance with a discussion between performers and audience in which the participants evaluate the presentation.

10. *Make a video*

Prepare a portion of a scene for a video production that you think could create a strong emotional impact on an audience. Consider the following questions before you make your video:

- Who will deliver the lines and present the actions?
- What emotion do you wish to focus on? How will you achieve the effect of the emotion?
- What camera angles will you use for each frame of your segment: close-up, medium close-up, or distance?
- How many shots will you use?
- What lighting effects might help to create the appropriate atmosphere?
- What music and other sound effects will you use?
- Show the complete video to your class.

11. Create a photo essay called "The Many Faces of Brutus." You might use images from old magazines, or take your own photos. Display your finished essay.

12. The characters Cassius, Brutus, Octavius, and Antony are all having dinner in a fancy Roman restaurant. During dinner, you overhear them discussing how their plans went awry after Caesar's assassination. How does each justify his actions and/or explain any "mistakes" he made? If each character were given a second chance, does he say he would have acted differently? Do you believe him? Record their conversation.

13. Play an in-class version of "Hollywood Squares" using questions on *Julius Caesar*. Arrange the desks into a tic-tac-toe pattern, and select nine "celebrities" and two contestants to compete for each square on the "board." Rotate "celebrities" so everyone has a chance to answer questions. You could also divide the entire class into nine groups, and have each group represent one square. Remember that part of the game is deciding whether a celebrity is giving the correct answer or is bluffing!

14. Organize a public forum in which a variety of experts assemble to discuss a number of issues raised by the play. Divide the class into the roles of opposing politicians, lawyers, famous journalists, and audience members, and choose someone to serve as the moderator or host of the discussion. The moderator times each speaker and keeps the discussion from straying from the stated topic. Using specific examples from the play to support your arguments, debate your views on the following statements:

   - "Power tends to corrupt; absolute power corrupts absolutely." (Lord Acton, 1888)
   - Many facets of heroism are examined in this play. Of the play's "heroes," including Pompey, Caesar, Brutus, Cassius, Antony, and Octavius, few actually act heroically. How should heroism be defined?

15. Create a board game or video game based on *Julius Caesar*. The idea is to win the most territory for Rome by moving around a map of the Roman Republic at the time of Caesar (approximately 44 B.C.E.). You are now a conquering Roman general, and you are at war. You win points whenever you capture a strategic territory. (You will have to research which were strategic territories at that time and which were not.) You lose points if your army is diverted, if your soldiers desert to another general, or worse, if you are defeated in battle. You have won the game when you have conquered everybody else and claimed their territories. Avoid such things as the following:

   - the Ides of any month
   - falling on your sword
   - seeing a ghost or encountering a soothsayer
   - making a bad strategic or military decision
   - listening to bad advice
   - thinking too long before making a move
   - trusting the wrong people
   - being in the wrong place at the wrong time
   - seeing omens that aren't favourable

You can add others as you invent strategies and complete your game. You might plan, design, and construct the board game or do a storyboard of a video game.